METHODIST DEVOTION

The Wesley Historical Society Lecture, No. 32
Methodist Conference, 1966
A Synopsis of which was delivered at
St. John's Methodist Church, Parkfield, Wolverhampton,
on Wednesday, 6th July

METHODIST DEVOTION

THE SPIRITUAL LIFE
IN THE METHODIST
TRADITION

1791–1945

GORDON S. WAKEFIELD

WIPF & STOCK · Eugene, Oregon

Wipf and Stock Publishers
199 W 8th Ave, Suite 3
Eugene, OR 97401

Methodist Devotion
The Spiritual Life in the Methodist Tradition, 1791-1945
By Wakefield, Gordon S.
Copyright©1966 Methodist Publishing - Epworth Press
ISBN 13: 978-1-5326-4638-6
Publication date 12/29/2017
Previously published by Epworth Press, 1966

CONTENTS

PREFACE   9

1. THE LEGACY FROM THE FIRST DAYS   13

2. NINETEENTH-CENTURY MODIFICATIONS   44

3. TWENTIETH-CENTURY TRIALS AND HOPES   89

4. EPILOGUE: COLLAPSE AND RENEWAL?   109

    INDEX   117

PREFACE

I⊤ is a great honour to have been asked to give the Wesley Historical Society's annual lecture, the more so, since, neither by temperament nor opportunity, am I to be numbered among those contributors to minute and meticulous scholarship, who are the Society's true *alumni* and by whom its real work is done. Yet, flirtatious as I have been, History was my academic first love, and I am particularly glad to be able to indulge yet further my interest in Christian Spirituality and, in some sense, to develop the theme of my Fernley-Hartley lecture for 1957, on *Puritan Devotion*.

This term 'Christian Spirituality' has become very fashionable, but requires definition. It derives from one of the classifications habitual to the Church of Rome, and formulated by M. l'Abbé Pourrat in his *La Spiritualité Chrétienne*. He distinguishes between 'Dogmatic', 'Moral', and 'Spiritual' Theology, and the greatest of these is Spiritual Theology, which is based upon the others, but is 'above them' in so far as it is a branch of the science which deals, not with abstract statements of faith and objective laws of conduct but with the life in Christ itself, the reality of that union with Him, which all traditions in some form would assert as the meaning of our salvation.

Today, the old-fashioned dichotomies of human nature are untenable. But the force of the term 'spiritual' does not lie in an invalid distinction between man's physical, earthly being and some supposed other part of him; rather, it recognizes that the means of union with Christ is God, the Holy Spirit. We pray in Him. He is the bond who, even as He unites the Father and the Son in the mysterious life of God, joins believers to their Head in the Body of Christ.

To attempt to describe and evaluate the prayer, discipline and hold on unseen realities of the Methodist people over a period of 150 years is a perilous task. To rely on printed sources alone would be unsatisfactory since we have to feel the pulse of a living movement. Imagination may help, but better still is personal memory of attitudes, devotion, and parental reminiscences. My mother used to tell me what life was like in the 1880s in a Methodist home of 'decent poverty'. I have in my possession a book of manuscript addresses given by her father to his Society Class in West Bromwich in the previous decade. Above all, I have myself the legacy of a Methodist upbringing, and a conscience, which, though often slighted and trampled on and somewhat enlarged with the years, remains, in the ground of my being, as Methodist as Charles Wesley's hymn

> *. . . a principle within*
> *Of jealous, godly fear,*
> *A sensibility of sin,*
> *A pain to feel it near*[1]

This would have been a better book had there been time for my friends in many communions to read and criticize it in advance. As it is, my indebtedness to others will be revealed in the footnotes, though it is simply not possible to compute, let alone acknowledge what I owe to the reading and conversations of years or to the privileged position of Connexional Editor, which enables me to see so much unpublished material. My work on the

---

[1] M.H.B. (1933) No. 626. Cf. the lines omitted from recent collections

> *And let me weep my life away*
> *For having grieved Thy love.*

biography of Dr R. Newton Flew, and access to his papers has also been of invaluable help and use.

I have drawn quite brazenly on a paper on *Private Devotion in the Methodist Tradition* read by the Rev. A. Raymond George to the World Council of Churches Faith and Order Commission and printed in *Studia Liturgica*, Volume II, Number 3, September 1963. He acknowledged so generously some comments which I made on his first draft as almost to make me feel that I had proprietary rights, but this, of course, is far from the case. I wish I had been able to avail myself of more of his impeccable scholarship than is contained in this invaluable article.

To my secretary, Miss Carolyn Deacon, I am grateful for help with the typescript, and also to my wife, without whose watchful care and ever-cheerful sharing of responsibility there would have been no book at all!

Harpenden   GORDON S. WAKEFIELD
Epiphany 1966

CHAPTER ONE

THE LEGACY FROM THE FIRST DAYS

THE TRAINING OF A METHODIST FORTY YEARS AGO

A FRAGMENT of autobiography may not seem the appropriate beginning to a supposedly learned work, but there is a very great danger that studies of the spiritual life may become, not simply abstract and divorced from the actual situation of the *plebs dei*, but descriptions of grand devotional designs which have no reality outside the textbooks. In an age in which Christians are beginning to be able to speak the truth in love about their own traditions as well as others, it would be particularly deplorable to seem to suggest that every Methodist society for a century and a half had ordered its life according to the ascetic doctrines of John Wesley or had even begun consciously to glimpse the full glories of his 'catholic spirit'. And so I start from what I myself received as a boy, growing up in a fairly large central church in a north-west industrial town. Its gleaming pitch-pine pews and galleries held one thousand people. By 1930 its leaders were already shaking their heads over the palpable decline in the numbers of worshippers, which they regarded as a somewhat delayed legacy of the 1914 war.

Of this Methodist Society, I was made a full member at baptism, and given a class ticket before my hands could hold one. There was no regular preparation for church membership until the late 1930s, and I myself underwent no ceremony of Christian initiation other than baptism. It is clear that the relation between church membership and any conscious 'decision for Christ' had not been thought out, but although the necessity of 'evangelical conversion' was implied in the tradition which the Church Fathers had themselves received, the majority of the members were rather squeamish about it, dubious about public appeals, frightened of emotionalism. In the 1930s, the Oxford Group Movement had its adherents among a few younger leaders who were clearly dissatisfied with what they felt was the Wesleyan complacency of the Church as a whole.

There may have been vestiges of a high doctrine of baptism in the Superintendent Minister's eagerness to count it as admission to the Society; more likely he was accepting the faith of the parents as sufficient for the child. Afterwards, a devout lady gave me a Bible, on the fly-leaf of which she had written out *A General Thanksgiving*, testimony, I think, to her Wesleyan love for the Prayer Book. Morning Prayer was never our custom; but I imagine that there was always a small minority who wished that it were. At any rate I was not allowed to escape its influence.

Any church member will, of course, select from the tradition of his local church those resources most congenial to his temperament and helpful to his notions of Christianity. The great spiritual gift of my church to me in boyhood was the hymn-book—the 1904 Wesleyan book, at first—which I devoured at the age of ten. In receiving this, it may be claimed, I received everything, 'a little body of experimental and practical divinity'—and, we may add mystical too. But already the true pattern of Wesleyan hymnody had been broken up and some of Charles Wesley mutilated, so that Bernard Manning in Cambridge was lamenting the 1904 compilation as a sad lapse into the commonplace after the glories of the original and nineteenth-century editions of 'A Collection of Hymns for the People Called Methodists'.[1] This meant that I was not made aware of Wesley's original table of contents, which reveal the book as a manual of evangelical experience for a society of converted and covenanted believers rather than an addition to the objective liturgy of the Church, though it must be remembered that the 1780 book presupposed the existence of the hymns for the Lord's Supper and the hymns for the festivals as well as the Book of Common Prayer. This was Wesley's original table:

Part I. containing Introductory Hymns
1. Exhorting and beseeching sinners to return to God.
2. Describing:
   i. The pleasantness of religion.
   ii. The goodness of God.
   iii. Death.
   iv. Judgement.
   v. Heaven.
   vi. Hell.
3. Praying for a blessing.

Part II
1. Describing formal Religion.
2. Describing inward Religion.

Part III
1. Praying for repentance.
2. Praying for mourners convinced of sin.
3. For mourners brought to the birth.
4. For persons convinced of backsliding.
5. For backsliders recovered.

---

[1] See Bernard L. Manning, *The Hymns of Wesley and Watts* (London 1942), pp. 7 ff.—a paper read to Cambridge University Methodist Society on 20 November, 1932.

Part IV
1. For believers rejoicing
2. For believers fighting
3. For believers praying
4. For believers watching
5. For believers working
6. For believers suffering
7. For believers groaning for full Redemption
8. For believers brought to the birth
9. For believers saved
10. For believers interceding for the world

Part V
1. For the Society meeting.
2. For the Society giving thanks.
3. For the Society praying.
4. For the Society parting.

This I did not then know. But I was conscious, perhaps through poring over the hymn-book in solitude, that much of Wesley was more suitable for private than for public use, and so I early joined the large company of Methodists who—as R. Newton Flew testified in very Methodist language—formed the habit 'of taking the *Hymn-book* into the secret place, where the soul prepares for the business of the day and freely talks with God'.[1]

It was thus that I became one of those who learnt to regard what follows as 'one of the unapproachable lyrics of devotion'[2] and 'an unspeakable treasure of the soul'.[3]

[1] R. Newton Flew, *The Hymns of Charles Wesley. A Study of their Structure* (London 1953), p. 9.

[2] R. Newton Flew, ibid., p. 70.

[3] J. Ernest Rattenbury, *The Evangelical Doctrines of Charles Wesley's Hymns* (London 1941), p. 184.

1. *Thou Shepherd of Israel, and mine,*
      The joy and desire of my heart,
   For closer communion I pine,
      I long to reside where Thou art:
   The pasture I languish to find
      Where all, who their Shepherd obey,
   Are fed, on Thy bosom reclined,
      And screened from the heat of day.

2. *Ah! show me that happiest place,*
      The place of Thy people's abode,
   Where saints in an ecstasy gaze,
      And hang on a crucified God;
   Thy love for a sinner declare,
      Thy passion and death on the tree;
   My spirit to Calvary bear,
      To suffer and triumph with Thee.

3. *'Tis there, with the lambs of Thy flock,*
      There only, I covet to rest,
   To lie at the foot of the rock,
      Or rise to be hid in Thy breast;
   'Tis there I would always abide,
      And never a moment depart,
   Concealed in the cleft of Thy side,
      Eternally held in Thy heart.

The hymn is, as the 1904 Wesleyan book indicated (but not, to its everlasting shame, the 1933 Methodist book), a meditation inspired by Song of Songs 1[7]: *Tell me, O thou whom my soul loveth, where thou feedest, where thou makest thy flock to rest at noon.*

Perhaps the most penetrating and poignant clue to interpretation is in the fact that the very mention of 'noon' in the text reminds Wesley of Calvary and that dread event when the midday sun was blotted out, and

yet which is the eternal rest and joy of the redeemed, and the secret of their union with God. John Preston, 'Prince Charles's Puritan Chaplain', in a moving soliloquy similarly inspired by *Canticles*, prays to Christ 'Show me where thou liest at this *my* noon',[1] which misses the overwhelming typological splendour of Wesley. Here, then, is Wesley bringing his own genius to mystical exegesis, and for the rest we cannot do better than refer to Dr Flew's commentary on the hymn in his Wesley Historical Society lecture on *The Hymns of Charles Wesley*. Flew claims that 'Charles Wesley in this lyric never goes beyond New Testament spirituality'. In Deissmann's famous distinction it is *com*munion rather than union which he celebrates: the bliss which he describes is shared with the other 'lambs of the flock'; and the object of devotion is eternally Christ Crucified.[2]

As to prayer in general, we were not given much guidance, though I have vague memories of a sermon by J. Arundel Chapman, probably in March 1930 before he went from the theology chair at Didsbury College to that at Headingley, in which he told of a man who would say the *Te Deum* to himself each morning as he shaved. I imagine that the sermon was about prayer as 'the practice of the presence of God' and would contain some very simple teaching about acts of recollection. I do not recall hearing anything quite like it until I began to listen to BBC religious talks from members of other communions.

Prayer was thought of as a private and personal activity not very clearly related to the Church or to public worship. Behind this apparent casualness and lack of help

[1] John Preston, *A Heavenly Treatise of Divine Love* (London 1640 edn.), pp. 89 ff. See G. S. Wakefield, 'Mysticism and its Puritan Types', *London Quarterly and Holborn Review*, January 1966, p. 40; *Puritan Devotion* (London 1957), p. 93. For a life of Preston see Irvonwy Morgan, *Prince Charles's Puritan Chaplain* (London 1957).   [2] Op. cit., pp. 69–74.

from the local Society in devotional practice, there was no doubt the belief that prayer was essentially the outpouring of a child's heart to his Father and required no elaborate technique. We used occasionally to sing James Montgomery's hymn:

> *Prayer is the simplest form of speech*
> *That infant lips can try.*[1]

It is easy to deplore this lack of systematic spirituality; but, despite the resulting impoverishment and defence-lessness, it had two beneficial and truly Methodist consequences. Prayer was not regarded as a difficult exercise about which we needed to develop scruples; and prayer was at best free and therefore extempore. The latter did not mean that to 'take the prayer' at a Guild or Class-meeting was not by far the hardest and most nerve-racking duty of the programme, but, even if, to begin with, some such support was required, it was not supposed to be beyond the capacity of any young person to write and read his, or more often her, prayer. This was entirely good.

Until the end of the 1930s, Holy Communion was administered about once a month, after the evening service. In his benediction to conclude the previous preaching service, one minister would say 'The grace of the Lord Jesus Christ, the Love of God, and the Fellow-ship of the Holy Spirit, be with us all—those who stay and those who go', which I suppose was a form of dismissal of catechumens, though I doubt if it was conceived as such. Communion was regarded as a solemn occasion, but I do

---

[1] *M.H.B.* 533. James Montgomery (1771–1854), editor of the *Sheffield Argus* and a renowned citizen of Sheffield, was a Moravian, whose relations with Methodism were always close, and who was a very distinguished hymnologist. From the memory of conversations with my father, I would opine that this hymn was sung in my home church more in the first twenty years of the century than from 1920–40.

not think there was much special private preparation for it. One young woman was once strongly rebuked by a cantankerous greybeard because she tripped out of the church vestibule to the Charleston or some such measure afterwards.

The 1933 hymn-book taught Methodists to sing William Bright's *And now O Father* at communion. It was used quite frequently, without, I imagine, much knowledge of its source, and probably because of the popularity of the tune *Unde et Memores* (how many of the congregation realized the significance of those words?), which was also sung to Samuel Greg's non-theological verses on the Transfiguration *Stay, Master, stay.*[1] Wesley's Eucharistic hymns were disregarded, and, for the most part unrecognized, since John Wesley had included several of them in other sections of the 1780 *Hymn-book*, and, since this was the collection which survived as the basis of subsequent books, their original purpose was forgotten. So, while we sang William Bright at the Sacrament without a qualm, we had no idea that Wesley's *O God of our Forefathers* with its crucial words:

> *With solemn faith we offer up*
> *And spread before Thy glorious eyes*
> *That only ground of all our hope*
> *That precious bleeding sacrifice*

had any relation to the Communion at all.

Visual aids in worship and prayer were absent. The crucifix was the badge of popery, and I, as a child, was much revolted by the tawdry and, sometimes, harrowing *pietà*, which strewed the home of some intimate Roman Catholic friends.

Class-meetings had become study or discussion groups,

[1] *Unde et memores* is, of course, from the Latin of the Great Prayer in the Roman Mass and the first verse of Bright's hymn (*M.H.B.* 759) is a paraphrase of the paragraph the words introduce.

in so far as they had not yielded place to the Wesley Guild, a more widely-educative means of fellowship. It had—and still has—as its aims, consecration, comradeship, citizenship and culture, and was then in its heyday.

The Annual Covenant Service, held, until the early 1930s, on the cold wintry afternoon of the first Sunday of the year, remained the distinctive Methodist rite, which many of the aged attended at great effort and personal expense. I can still hear the hoary octogenarians bursting into Philip Doddridge's *O Happy Day* with its later chorus, as they returned from the Lord's Table. Then came the new version, much of it by G. B. Robson and John Hunter, and this was relegated to an after-service on Sunday night, though, in all fairness, it must be said that this probably meant more participants.[1]

Love Feasts lingered in the memory of my elders, but I never attended one. Prayer meetings were revived first by the Groupers, then at the outbreak of World War II, but, for the most part, they were quiet and devout, and lacking in fervour. In the Circuit, there were societies with more of the corybantic legacy of earlier Methodism, one, where on my visits as a young local preacher, prayers and sermon would be punctuated with alleluias and amens. Cliff College had its outposts and its influence, which reminded us of a type of spirituality which had nothing to do but to save souls, and lead them on to claim the 'second blessing' of entire sanctification. I do not myself recall any sermon even at the time of the bicentenary of Wesley's evangelical conversion in 1938, which taught me much about 'our doctrines' as distinct from a general, often rather liberal Christianity, or the occasional aggressive appeal for decision which won admiration for the preacher's sincerity rather than converts. For these I

[1] See David Tripp, 'A Revised Covenant Service', *London Quarterly and Holborn Review*, January 1966.

had to wait until I read Wesley for examinations. But, in retrospect, the spirituality of my church was poised uneasily between a rigid logic of evangelical conversion, which did not seem to fit all cases, an anxiety to be relevant to a world which was clearly very different from the previous two centuries, and an intermittent longing for a richer and more Catholic heritage, which seemed at times to be glimpsed through the Wesley hymns. To some extent, this dilemma was the result of the manifoldness of Wesley's own experience.

THE MULTI-PATTERNED SPIRITUALITY OF THE WESLEYS

There is disagreement among scholars as to which were the decisive influences on Wesley's own spirituality. His Epworth home itself united many strains. His conversion in the sense of dedication to serious Christianity, which took place in 1725, was due to the Caroline Jeremy Taylor, the medieval Thomas à Kempis, and the Non-Juror William Law. Oxford and Georgia saw him High Anglican and mystical. Yet it was German pietism which brought him to Aldersgate Street and assurance, and which released his energies for the conversion of England, and, temporarily, made him feel that his previous masters had led him along the road to Sinai if not to Egypt. When he edited *The Christian Library* for his preachers, he chose more extracts from the English Puritans than from anywhere else thus returning to the inspiration of his grandparents. Yet Outler has brilliantly shown the links between Wesley and the Greek Fathers' understanding of Christian perfection, and Orcibal has uncovered the underground ecumenical movement[1] by which continental

[1] Albert C. Outler (ed.), *John Wesley*, The Library of Protestant Thought (O.U.P., New York 1964).

Jean Orcibal, 'The Theological Originality of John Wesley and Continental Spirituality' in Rupert Davies and Gordon Rupp (eds.) *A History of the Methodist Church in Great Britain*, Vol. I, (London 1966), pp. 81 ff.

spirituality and English fertilized each other. What is more, Wesley's anti-mysticism did not wholly persist and for the last thirty years of his long life it seems as though there was little of his past that he would repudiate.

Charles Wesley's story is similar for some years but he was more rapturous and less restrained, which led him into a happy marriage, and by the inevitable reaction to which such a psychology is prone, to a greater conformity, Anglican and social, at the last. He believed fervently in evangelical conversion, but came to regard perfect love in this life as an aspiration rather than a possibility.[1]

It will be well for us to try to illustrate the various elements of the Wesleys' spirituality, and then to decide which was in fact the most normative in the continuing life of the Methodist people, who, it is important to remember, were not simply Wesley creations.

NATIVE ANGLICANISM

It is, as everyone knows, impossible to understand Wesley apart from the Church of England which nurtured him, and to which his parents had both turned, although their fathers had suffered in the dissenting cause. Wesley gave to Methodism the Book of Common Prayer, and it was more loved in itself than his 1784 abridgement. He did not envisage his people existing without Morning Prayer and the 1662 Order for Holy Communion. He did, however, seem to regard the former as, principally, a Sunday Service. At any rate, whatever his own practice, Methodists as a whole have not looked upon Morning and Evening Prayer as orders for *daily* use. On the other hand, Wesley continued to republish his Oxford *Collection of Forms of Prayer for Every Day in the Week*, and was clearly determined that free prayer both private and public should be

[1] See H. A. Hodges and A. M. Allchin, *A Rapture of Praise*, (London 1966), p. 27.

disciplined by the sound patterns of the liturgical tradition. In these forms, he was much influenced by the Non-Jurors—Robert Nelson, Nathaniel Spinckes, Thomas Ken, as well as John Donne and the Carolines. Anglicanism gave him his knowledge of and love for the early Fathers, and, through Jeremy Taylor and William Law, brought him to his first conversion at Oxford: 'In the year 1725, being in the twenty-third year of my age, I met with Bishop Taylor's *Rules and Exercises of Holy Living and Dying*. In reading several parts of this book, I was exceedingly affected by that part in particular which referred to 'purity of intention'. Instantly I resolved to dedicate *all my life* to God, *all* my thoughts and words and actions, being thoroughly convinced there was no medium but that *every* part of my life (not *some* only) must either be a sacrifice to God or to myself; that is, in effect, to the devil. . . .'[1] Hence sprang his ordered life, his fasting, which he and his followers regarded as a most important discipline, and his good works.

Anglican, too, is his trust in reason, source of his 'calm appeals' and of his own calm amid all the emotional storms around him, his readiness to argue and controvert, his scorn of the 'namby-pambical'. He fits Howard Johnson's account of the Broad Churchman, at the Toronto Conference of 1963:

'He is the liberal. He is not necessarily the political liberal; not even (in an opprobrious sense) the theological liberal. He is someone who learned from Richard Hooker and the Caroline Divines the importance of *reason*. He acknowledges that there may be elements in revelation which are *supra rationem* (above reason). He resists, however, anything which is *contra rationem* (against reason).'[2]

Not least is Wesley Anglican in his rediscovery, though

[1] *Works*, XI, 366.
[2] *Anglican Congress: Report of Proceedings* (London 1964), pp. 231–2.

only after his encouter with the Moravians, of the reality of justification by faith. His evangelical conversion in May 1738 and its consequences thrust him back upon the Anglican *Homilies*, those comprehensively Protestant and Scriptural documents from which he published an extract before the end of 1738. It was Anglicanism which saved him from the confusion of 'faith' with 'feeling', and which helped him to understand so clearly that personal religion is upheld and sustained and, indeed, engendered by the Eucharist, so that his evangelical revival became a sacramental revival too, and he and his brother bequeathed for the celebrations of the Methodists and the devotions of future generations, the *Hymns on the Lord's Supper*. Bear in mind, also, the traditional Anglican veneration for the Fathers, and that Puritan moral theology, at any rate, has close links with Anglican and we may be content to assess Wesley himself as *anima naturaliter Anglicana;* but this is not to make the same judgement upon his followers.

THE CATHOLIC STRAIN

Wesley believed that the nearer in time one came to the Gospel events, the purer the religion. He revered the ante-Nicene Fathers, and regarded a knowledge of them as among the chief privileges of a university education.[1] He was not blind to their faults and weaknesses. In his letter to Dr Conyers Middleton he compared them to some of his own early Methodists. They were not gifted with great learning, at times they argued their case badly but 'they were Christians' and their writings 'describe true, genuine Christianity'.[2]

[1] Cf. 'Address to the Clergy' (1756) *Works*, X, 484.
[2] See 'A Letter to the Reverend Doctor Conyers Middleton, occasioned by His Late Free Enquiry', *Works*, X, pp. 1-79.
Also Albert C. Outler (ed.), *John Wesley* (Library of Protestant Thought) (Oxford, New York 1964), p. 195.

One of these Fathers was known as 'Macarius the Egyptian' and Wesley included extracts from his homilies in the first volume of *The Christian Library*. Recent scholarship has established that this 'Macarius' was no Egyptian 'desert father' but a fifth-century *Syrian* monk, whose conception of Christian spirituality was derived almost entirely from Gregory of Nyssa, 'the greatest of all the Eastern teachers of the quest for perfection'.[1] This means that the young Wesley was influenced by Orthodox monasticism and that his teaching about perfection was thereby freed from certain of the Roman and sectarian *faux pas*. Perfection for him was never a moral state which could not be improved, it was a life of constant growth in disciplined love to God and man. To quote 'Macarius' 'It is only gradually that a man grows and comes to *a perfect man, to the measure of the stature*, not as some say, "Off with one coat and on with another".'[2]

Wesley also admired the later Fathers of both East and West 'St Chrysostom, Basil, Jerome, Austin, and, above all, that man of a broken heart Ephraim Syrus'.[3] Ephraem Syrus (*c.* 306–373), saint and scholar, had a legendary reputation in the Middle East and Edessa. He had a great devotion to the Blessed Virgin and some of his theology would be uncongenial to twentieth-century Protestants. He does, however, belong to the Eastern school of perfectionism, like 'Macarius', and much of his

[1] Albert C. Outler, ibid. See pp. 9, 10, particularly note 26 to which this paragraph is indebted. R. N. Flew, *The Idea of Perfection in Christian Theology* (Oxford 1934) chapter VIII has a valuable summary of the teaching of the homilies which is not undermined by discoveries of later scholarship as to their provenance.

[2] *Homilies* (ed. A. J. Mason 1921), 15, 51. See the very important discussions in Outler, *John Wesley*, p. 31, and H. A. Hodges and A. M. Allchin, *A Rapture of Praise*, pp. 18–30.

[3] *Works*, X, 484. 'It is interesting to notice the quality in Ephraem which particularly attracts him'—A. M. Allchin in *We belong to One Another* (London 1965), p. 68.

teaching is in the form of hymns and sacred poems, which would doubtless be an added attraction for the Wesleys.

But the Catholic strain in Wesley's spirituality joins him to the Western Church as well as the Eastern, to the Middle Ages as well as the Patristic period, to Rome as well as to Canterbury. Years ago, Bernard Manning pointed out the comparison between some of Wesley hymns and the medieval cult of the five wounds of Jesus.

> *Five bleeding wounds He bears*
> *Received on Calvary;*
> *They pour effectual prayers,*
> *They strongly speak for me.*[1]

There may be some dispute as to how far this language can be supported from the New Testament, though it is always dangerous to accuse Wesley of being unscriptural. It reminds us, at any rate, that as James Moffatt magnificently wrote, Christ's 'intercession . . . has red blood in it';[2] and the wounds are not the 'dumb mouths' of Anthony's speech over the corpse of Caesar, they belong to one who is alive and victorious yet whose scars are eternally fresh because his heart is eternally tender. He is never as though he had *not* suffered. His love would always go to the Cross for sinners. In a classic statement Methodist preaching is defined by Wesley as:

> To invite, to convince, to offer Christ . . . to preach him in
> all his offices . . . *to set forth Christ as evidently crucified before*

---

[1] *M.H.B.* 368, cf. 319, 365; also many references to the pierced hands and open side. See Bernard Manning, *The Hymns of Wesley and Watts* (London 1942), p. 133.

[2] James Moffatt, *I.C.C. Commentary on Hebrews 19*, p. 100, quoted by E. G. Rupp in a paper, read to the 1965 Oxford Institute of Methodist Studies on 'The Finished Work of Christ in Word and Sacrament', at present unpublished and to which the paragraph is indebted. This modifies slightly what I wrote in *New Directions*, Vol. 2, No. 5, p. 27, though see Franz Hildebrandt's forthcoming *I Offered Christ* for a different view.

their eyes, justifying us by his blood and sanctifying us by his spirit.[1]

There is no difference between this and Pusey's assertion that Christian spirituality is to keep the cross ever before our eyes.[2]

Wholly Scriptural or no, this piety of the Crucified is altogether Anglo-Saxon,[3] and it has undoubted affinities with the 'shewings' of Julian of Norwich and may be relieved of its stark horror and crudity if it is interpreted by a discerning sentence of Dom David Knowles writing of the fourteenth-century English mystic 'The bodily sight does little more than release a deeper shewing in the understanding.'[4] It is a pity that the Wesleys, sharing the ignorance of their age, did not know the medieval mystics. This tenderness and compassion in the spirituality of the Wesleys, which draws John alike to Ephraem Syrus and a Crucified Saviour is, again, very English, at least until the middle of the nineteenth century. 'The water', as Bunyan would say, often stood in the Puritan's eyes—witness Oliver Cromwell.[5] And Lancelot Andrewes' manuscript of the *Preces Privatae* was 'slubbered with his pious hands and watered with his penitential tears'.[6] But A.M. Allchin has compared Methodist with Byzantine piety at this point. Symeon the new Theologian preached

[1] There is a similar sentiment in one of the Eucharistic Hymns:

> *Crucified before our eyes*
> *Where we our Maker see.*

(Eucharistic hymns 21 : *M.H.B.* 191.)

[2] E. B. Pusey: *Sermon at the opening of the Chapel of Keble College* (1876), p. 31.

[3] See Charles Smyth, *The Church and the Nation* (London 1962), pp. 36–8.

[4] David Knowles, *The English Mystical Tradition* (1961), p. 124.

[5] E.g. his parting with George Fox, the Quaker as described in G. Fox, *Journal*, ed. N. Penney, I, pp. 167 f.

[6] Richard Drake in his Preface to his translation of the *Preces*, 1648, quoted by F. E. Brightman, *The Preces Privatae of Lancelot Andrewes* (London 1903).

of the need of the heart of stone to become 'a well of tears'. We may recall Charles Wesley in

> *Stone to flesh again convert*
> *Cast a look, and break my heart.*[1]

Symeon also counselled in the words of his own spiritual father, Symeon the Pious, 'Brother, never communicate without tears'. Allchin puts beside this two fine and moving passages from J. E. Rattenbury's *The Evangelical Doctrines of Charles Wesley's Hymns:* 'Adoring pentitents, Charles Wesley or Fra Angelico, arrive at the very heart of truth by cries and tears, penitence and adoration', and again 'It may still . . . be questioned whether any lenses have yet been constructed as perfect for visualizing Jesus as penitent tears, Charles Wesley shed many, which, though they dimmed his sight, clarified his vision.'[2] At any rate, in the full version of his great hymn on *Conscience*, Wesley prays

> *And let me weep my life away*
> *For having grieved Thy love.*[3]

But we must not exaggerate Wesley's distinctiveness here. At a time when the whole House of Commons could dissolve into tears, he was not exceptional.

Behind this, there is, of course, the understanding, basic to all Christian Spirituality, that however near to the heights of perfection the believer, through God's grace may come, he never outgrows the lowly prayer of the publican from which he started: 'God be merciful to me'.[4]

Wesley was well aware that serious religion could

---

[1] *M.H.B.* 348.

[2] Rattenbury, op. cit., pp. 101, 158.
See A. M. Allchin, *We belong to One Another*, pp. 71 ff.

[3] The hymn *I want a principle within* is No. 626 in the 1933 *M.H.B.*, but these lines have been excluded since 1904.

[4] Cf. *M.H.B.* 348. For further links here with Eastern piety cf. H. A. Hodges, Introduction to E. Kadloubovsky, *Unseen Warfare* (London 1952).

transcend confessional divisions and he wished to join hands with all those dedicated to the unremitting pursuit of holiness. On his continental journeying to Herrnhut in the summer of 1738 he noticed with approval how much better the Catholics observed the outward forms of religion than the Protestants. They said their morning prayer (with bared heads) on the Rhine boat and never took the name of God in vain or scoffed at religion.[1] His open *Letter to a Roman Catholic* written at the end of his third visit to Dublin in 1749 is a remarkably ecumenical document in that age of religious and political mistrust. It draws on his favourite distinction—Anglican and in no sense original—between essential beliefs and mere opinions, and on his understanding, rediscovered as one of the signal insights of the Nottingham Faith and Order Conference of 1964, that, as Outler comments, the difficulties could be discussed more fruitfully within the potential community of faith and love in the actual situation of estrangement.[2] But the burden of the letter is that 'the old religion' of faith working by love, 'true, primitive Christianity', belongs both to Roman Catholics and those 'commonly called Protestants'.

Wesley had felt that there was genuine evidence of this in the piety of the Counter-Reformation. It is unfortunate that he was not able to study the great Carmelites at first hand and that, for him, the paragons of Roman sanctity were the Frenchman, M. de Renty, and the Mexican hermit, Gregory Lopez, neither of whom, as Rupp points out, 'has been canonized by his Church'.[3] Wesley

[1] *Journal*, II, 6, 7.

[2] Cf. Albert C. Outler, *John Wesley* (Library of Protestant Thought), pp. 492–3. The letter is printed on pp. 493 ff. of that collection. It is found in *Works*, X, pp. 80–6. For the Nottingham Conference see the resolution on pp. 58–61, 75 of *Unity Begins at Home* (London 1964).

[3] Gordon Rupp, *A History of the Methodist Church in Great Britain*, Vol. I, p. xxxi.

included abridged lives of these two in *The Christian Library*. Gregory Lopez (1542–96) was a Spaniard, born in Madrid, who went out to Mexico and from the age of twenty dedicated himself entirely to the pursuit of salvation. He lived as a recluse on a frugal diet, in a room which contained only a Bible, a globe and a pair of compasses, though he managed to master the works of St Teresa in twenty hours. His knowledge of the Bible became (not unnaturally) phenomenal, and although at first his private enterprise piety and his absence from mass made the hierarchy suspicious, he was renowned in · his generation for supernatural wisdom and the pure love of God. Wesley was haunted by Lopez. He was not blind to his limitations. He refers to him as 'that good and wise, tho' much mistaken man'.[1] But what Wesley never forgot was that Lopez's life became constant prayer, though Wesley realized that this was to put the matter in the lowest terms. What Lopez experienced was 'an open intercourse' with God, 'a close, uninterrupted communion'.[2]

Count Gaston Jean-Baptiste de Renty (1611–49), a French nobleman, lived in Paris and was married, although he seems to have learnt a holy detachment from his wife as well as from his wealth. He founded in Paris a society of ladies for what was virtually the perpetual adoration of the Blessed Sacrament. He combined mysticism with philanthropy in a remarkable way. He was at once intensely dedicated, writing out a covenant with Christ in his own blood, penetrating by contemplation into the mysteries of the Holy Trinity, and yet caring for the sick, the aged, the exiled and gathering around him groups of Christians, which Henry Bett regarded as the true precursors of the Methodist class-meeting,[3]

[1] *Journal*, 31/8/42.   [2] See, e.g. *Letters*, V, 283.
[3] See Henry Bett, *Wesley Historical Society Proceedings*, 1931, pp. 41 ff.

rather than the 'Religious Societies' of London or the 'Collegia Pietatis' of Germany.

There is no doubt that Wesley was attracted by the 'massive heroism' of Counter-Reformation spirituality. There is at times something almost frightening about his own austerity and wish to be free from the ordinary concerns of human life. Within two months of his death he wrote to Adam Clarke who had just lost a child: 'But you startle me when you talk of grieving so much for the death of an infant. This was certainly a proof of inordinate affection; and if you love them thus all your children will die. How did Mr de Renty behave when he supposed his wife to be dying? This is a pattern for a Christian.'[1]

It was not for nothing that he translated Antoinette Bourignon's hymn

> *Empty my heart of earthly love,*
> *And for Thyself prepare the place.*

WESLEY AND MYSTICISM[2]

There is no doubt that during and after the struggles towards his evangelical conversion, Wesley felt that he had been betrayed by 'the mystic writers, whose noble descriptions of union with God and internal religion made everything else appear mean, flat and insipid'.[3] By these writers he seems to have meant a very mixed company including William Law, Michael Molinos, Fénelon, Francke, de Renty, François de Sales, Madame Guyon

[1] *Letters*, VIII, 253.

[2] D. Dunn Wilson has completed a thesis on this subject. There is published treatment in the Wesley chapters of R. A. Knox, *Enthusiasm* (Oxford 1950), Martin Schmidt, *John Wesley* (London 1962), and most recently on pp. 374–6 of H. Jaeger's chapter 'La Mystique Protestante et Anglicane' of *La Mystique et Les Mystiques* (Brussels 1965), Jean Orcibal's chapter in *A History of the Methodist Church in Great Britain*, A. C. Outler (ed.), *John Wesley*, and H. A. Hodges and A. M. Allchin, *A Rapture of Praise*.

[3] Wesley, as in Outler, pp. 46–7.

and the *Theologia Germanica*. In the despondency of the
Georgian crisis he came to think that their teaching
undermined faith, works and reason equally, and con-
demned the soul to a lone struggle through the dark
wilderness of solitary, introspective religion, with no
means of grace to be guide posts and no pilgrim song of
assurance to speed the way. His language was vehement
at this period. 'All the other enemies of Christianity are
triflers—the mystics are the most dangerous of its enemies.'
Ironically, the Moravians, who had pointed him to
justification by faith alone, and thereby to the English
Reformers, and away from the Behmenist syncretism of
William Law, proved to be the most dangerously mystical
of all in their quietist disavowal of the sacraments. It was
controversy with them which in 1743 provoked Wesley
to his most intemperate language against the mystic
writers 'whom I declare in my cool judgement and in the
presence of the Most High God, I believe to be the one
great anti-Christ'. Wesley never took kindly to the more
mystical hymns of his brother, and omitted *Thou Shepherd
of Israel and mine* from the 1780 *Hymn-book*, not apparently
being as convinced of its safeguards as Dr Flew! His
sermon on *The Wilderness State* seems in part to be an
attack on the mystic doctrine of 'the dark night of the
soul'.

Yet once controversy had abated and he was able to
see the crisis of his own conversion in focus, Wesley
tempered some of his criticisms. From 1765 he deleted
the sentence about 'anti-Christ' from all editions of his
journal. He was willing for his preachers to read some of
the mystic writers. He taught Methodists to sing his
translation of Paul Gerhardt and of Tersteegen, and
there are signs that the influence of John Fletcher helped
him to evaluate the mystics more justly. In Letter V to
Richard Hill, in the fourth of his *Checks to Antiromianism*,

Fletcher distinguishes between false mysticism and the true mysticism of Scripture, which furthers 'the deep mysteries of inward religion', and hopes that, in future, Mr Wesley will do the same.[1]

Whatever the fluctuations of John Wesley, the hymns of Charles, who in any case never reacted so violently against the mystic writers, are sufficient witness that in its broader sense of longing for immediacy of communion with God, mysticism has its place in Methodist spirituality. The very fervour and intensity of the movement, its protection against cold, formal outward religion guarantees that. It is a matter of distinguishing with Fletcher, between different kinds of mysticism, between various aberrations of the middle ages, the Counter-Reformation and pietism and the great traditions of West and East in both of which we may now assert that Wesley stood. There is no difficulty in associating Wesley with the *Western Mysticism* which Dom Cuthbert Butler describes in his great book of that title,[2] a mysticism which is not pseudo-Dionysian so much as in the grand succession of Augustine, Gregory and Bernard. To this we must add those Eastern influences, by which Outler sets such store.[3] In any case, no man who wrote as John Wesley did—in 1771 be it noted—about Gregory Lopez can be written off as an anti-mystic. The whole extract is important, not only because of Wesley's own language and attitude, but because of what it discloses about our main subject, the spirituality of the Methodist people:

A continual desire is a continual prayer—that is, in a low sense of the word; for there is a far higher sense such an

[1] See John Fletcher, *Works*, 4 vols. (New York 1854), I, 238. Cf. J. Orcibal, in Davies and Rupp, *A History of the Methodist Church in Great Britain*, p. 96.

[2] First edition London 1922, second edition London 1926.

[3] See Outler, *John Wesley*, pp. 63–4, for a clear distinction between the various types of mysticism which influenced Wesley.

open intercourse with God, such a close uninterrupted communion with Him, as Gregory Lopez experienced, and not a few of our brethren and sisters now alive.[1]

We may describe Methodism as *prophetic mysticism*, thus combining the two terms of Frederick Heiler's famous distinction between mystical and prophetic prayer.[2] It was the mysticism of the Old Testament prophets—an immediacy of communion with God, realized in the sheer, ardent rapture of response to His mighty acts of grace.[3] There is an account of the aged Wesley himself after a sermon at City Road remaining for ten minutes in the perfect silence of intense communion with God, 'His eyes were closed, his countenance devoutly lifted to heaven, and his hands clasped together on the pulpit Bible'.[4] It is somewhat reminiscent of St Francis of Assisi at Averna 'uplifted towards God in seraphic ardour of desire'. But Wesley received no stigmata; neither was his rapture in a flight of the alone to the Alone, for he went on to announce his brother's hymn 'Come let us join our friends above'. Clearly, he had been with the whole company of heaven, yet it is no abuse of language to regard this as a mystical experience.

Wesley taught his followers meditation, and for this went to Puritan models. He regarded meditation as one of the 'instituted' means of grace and, in an alternative version of his advice to helpers, wrote 'Meditating: At set times? How? By Bishop Hall's or Mr Baxter's rule

[1] *Letters*, V, 283.
[2] F. Heiler, *Prayer* (many English editions from London 1932). Heiler admits that the division into types is a scientific construction, which does not do justice to all individual manifestations.
[3] Cf. E. J. Tinsley's reference to Lindblom's phrase about 'the concentration ecstasy' of the Hebrew Prophets, 'The Bible and Mysticism', *York Quarterly*, November 1957.
[4] See L. F. Church, *More About the Early Methodist People* (London 1949), p. 220.

How long?'[1] Wesley included extracts from both these authors in *The Christian Library*. Neither of them, of course, was tinged with the type of mysticism which he deplored. Both are steeped in the Augustinian and Bernardine tradition.

Baxter in *The Saints' Everlasting Rest*[2] gives a lengthy account of Set or Solemn Meditation. This begins with *Consideration* or *Cogitation*, active spiritual reasoning. The matter on which this must work is produced by the memory (doubtless aided by a notebook!) which furnishes suitable scripture passages and promises, articles of the creed, or extracts from spiritual writings. These should be stored over the years. The judgement then examines the promise contained in the passage chosen. This will often result in questioning and argument in order to bring conviction of the truth of Scripture or tradition, but the mind's assent to this must be turned into positive and personal assurance, that the general promise of God is all related to *my* everlasting joy.

Next, the affections must be kindled in love, desire, hope, courage and joy—all to be inflamed by consideration of the chosen passage. And so we pass to a further stage, *Soliloquy*, 'which is nothing but a pleading the case with our own souls', 'a preaching to one's self'. This is likely to lead to reproof and penitence and prayer, speaking sometimes to ourselves and sometimes to God. (The Psalms are patterns of soliloquy.) Prayer 'which is a weightier duty than most are aware of' is the climax of meditation.

This careful and solemn exercise will obviously lead sometimes to an 'ecstatic pause' as we glimpse something of the glories of the Kingdom of God. But special insights

[1] *Minutes of the Methodist Conference*, London 1812, p. 17.
[2] The latest edition of this is the one edited and abridged by John T. Wilkinson (London 1962), which has been used in this summary.

and graces apart, it will help us towards that goal which Charles Wesley desired:

> *O that my every breath were praise!*
> *O that my heart were filled with God!*[1]

It may at times end in aridity and heaviness; of this Wesley was not perhaps sufficiently aware. John Haime, one of his 'veterans', after three years of conscious communion with God, passed through a period of despair which lasted for twenty. Wesley was puzzled by this, as a Catholic would not have been.[2]

Some might feel that Baxter's meditation is too cerebral and demands intellectual activity beyond the capacity of simpler folk. Meditation, for him, comprehends consideration and contemplation.[3] Perhaps it would have been appropriate to the genius of Methodism had it been able to regard contemplation as not inevitably the result of meditation, and therefore the crown of long mental effort, but as the simple surrender of the soul to God in the ground of our being.[4]

BASIC PURITANISM

We have already been compelled to refer to Wesley's dependence on the Puritans. The logic of his preaching, his utter seriousness, as well as his suggested revisions of the Book of Common Prayer were all Puritan.

Some years ago, in the Fernley-Hartley Lecture for 1957, I tried to show that Puritan spirituality is much more catholic and comprehensive than has been imagined, and that we err grievously if we think of the Puritans as

---

[1] *M.H.B.* 452.

[2] See John Telford (ed.), *Wesley's Veterans* (London 1912–14). At least one Jesuit was denied 'consolations' for a similar period.

[3] J. T. Wilkinson (ed.), *The Saints' Everlasting Rest*, p. 140.

[4] Cf. A. M. Ramsey, *Sacred and Secular* (London 1965), Chapter 3, particularly p. 45.

humourless kill-joys, harsh and negative, latter-day Manicheans.[1] It is not easy to differentiate Puritan from genuine Christian spirituality of any kind, any more than it is to describe true Methodism as other than the plain religion of the New Testament. Most of our analysis so far of the various strains of Wesley's teaching could apply to the innumerable manuals of Puritan piety, Calvinist, though many of the Puritans were, while even Wesley's perfectionism is not essentially different in his definitive treatises, from that of John Preston. George Croft Cell's dictum that Wesley's teaching was 'the necessary synthesis of the Protestant ethic of grace and the Catholic ethic of holiness' is still very fashionable;[2] but it could be applied without gross exaggeration to the Puritans, in spite of 'the pessimism of grace' and the fact that they did not sing of perfect love so loud.

Yet the delights and spiritual benefits of singing are anticipated in Baxter as are the hymns themselves in Watts and Doddridge (and specifically Sacramental hymns in these and in Joseph Stennett the Baptist). We might almost say without too lamentable an imprecision that Methodism was simply English Puritanism in a less intellectual and more popular and altogether Arminian form.

And it was certain peculiarly Puritan emphases which governed the developing ethos of Methodism for the century after Wesley's death. From the Puritans, Joseph and Richard Alleine, Wesley derived the Covenant Service. He made a private custom into a congregational act, but like the Puritans, the early Methodists made their own special and personal covenants with God.[3] On the other

---

[1] See my *Puritan Devotion* (London 1957).

[2] G. C. Cell, *John Wesley's Theology* (Nashville, Tennessee 1950), pp. 361 ff.

[3] E.g. L. F. Church, *More About the Early Methodist People*, pp. 274 ff.

hand, so did M. de Renty, and we may err if we imagine that Federal Theology is exclusively Calvinist, Puritan, or even evangelical.[1] The habit of keeping journals, which persisted well into the nineteenth century, was Puritan, though, again, not exclusively so. So was the belief in the family as a Church, and of the importance of family prayers. So was the expectation that prayer might often, though not exclusively, be without book or set form. So was the honouring of the Lord's Day, and the great place accorded to the sermon in worship.

In other respects did the Methodists' debt to Puritanism accumulate interest in subsequent years. One was the belief in the necessity of evangelical conversion, though the term is not Puritan any more than it is Wesley's. Puritanism was not a movement of mass evangelism or revivalism, but the story of young Thomas Goodwin at Christ's, Cambridge, and the agonies of his struggle for assurance was of a pattern with that of the young Thomas Collins, 200 years later and in a Warwickshire town. The training and making tender of conscience from earliest years was both Puritan and Methodist. Susanna Wesley brought up her large family on Puritan principles[2] and so did Methodists after her for more than two centuries.

Not least important, Methodist spirituality, like Puritan, eschewed visual aids. It had in its hymns and preaching a crucifix in the sense of the 'Shakespeare of the Puritans', Thomas Adams, 'a faire and lively crucifixe, cut by the hande of a most exquisite carver; not to amaze our corporall lights with a peece of wood, brasse, or stone curiously engraven to the increase of a carnall devotion. But to present to the eye of the conscience the grievous passion and most gracious compassion of our Saviour

[1] If it comes to that, the words of the Covenant may be paralleled in the Ignatian Exercises.
[2] See John A. Newton, *Methodism and the Puritans* (London 1964).

Jesus Christ.'[1] The Methodist did not really think to enter the Kingdom by eye-gate.

But what is it, which gives this synthesis a vitality of its own, which makes it *Methodist*, vulgar, yet sober, not just Puritan or Anglican but 'a somehow deviating Protestant group, with a drop of Catholic tradition still in their blood'.[2] Perhaps it is the note of cheerfulness which is the distinguishing mark of Methodist spirituality. As Martin Schmidt has written:

> One of John Wesley's favourite expressions was the equation: holiness is happiness. This association of the impulse towards holiness with joy in salvation, which is a characteristic of Methodism as a whole, is to be found very early in Wesley, and is the demonstrable constant in all his theological statements. It is rooted in a long English tradition.[3]

Schmidt goes on in a footnote to list many Puritan and Anglican works. He might have gone further back still to Margery Kempe or Julian of Norwich in the fourteenth century: 'all shall be well and all shall be well and all manner of thing shall be well.'[4]

This was why Wesley mistrusted 'the dark night of the soul'; why he disliked solitary religion so much, in spite of his admiration for Lopez and the desert. 'There is no holiness but social holiness.'

---

[1] *Works* (1630), p. 817.

[2] Paul Tillich, *Ultimate Concern* (London 1965), p. 91.

[3] Martin Schmidt, *John Wesley*, Vol. I, p. 308. Sometimes his preachers needed to be rebuked for preaching—as is a constant temptation—more of fear than of joy.

[4] Cf. Martin Thornton, *English Spirituality* (London 1963), p. 49; also *Margery Kempe* (London 1960).

Not in the tombs we pine to dwell
Not in the dark monastic cell
By vows and grates confined
Freely to all ourselves we give,
Constrained by Jesu's love to live
The servants of mankind.

The Love Feast, taken over from the Moravians at Herrnhut, and looking back towards the primitive *Agape*, was a symbol of this social holiness. Biscuits and water were eaten and drunk and testimony given to what God had done in believer's hearts and lives. The class-meeting was a signal means of its nurture. Here spiritual direction was given in the group and the members were to care for one another and lead one another to deeper experience of God's love and fresh progress towards 'the height of holiness'. Our modern hymn-books do not allow us to see that the Wesley hymn *Help us to help each other Lord* is a truncated version of a hymn about the examination of the soul, which presupposes the class-meeting.

1. *Try us, O God, and search the ground*
   Of every sinful heart:
   Whate'er of sin in us is found,
   O bid it all depart!

2. *When to the right or left we stray,*
   Leave us not comfortless!
   But guide our feet into the way
   Of everlasting peace.

3. *Help us to help each other, Lord,*
   Each other's cross to bear,
   Let each his friendly aid afford,
   And feel his brother's care.

4. *Help us to build each other up,*
   Our little stock improve;
   Increase our faith, confirm our hope,
   And perfect us in love.

5. *Up into thee our living Head,*
   Let us in all things grow,
   Till thou hast made us free indeed,
   And spotless here below.

6. *Then, when the mighty work is wrought,*
   Receive thy ready Bride;
   Give us in heav'n a happy lot
   With all the sanctified.

Heart-searching was no lonely introspection: it was a group activity, and doubtless took place in depth, if not in the classes, in the bands, smaller and select companies of the most earnest members. Wesley saw no analogy between this and 'Popish confession'. He was right in that there was no sacerdotalism, no danger of tyranny. But its purpose was what that of confession should be—spiritual guidance, strengthening and help. Wesley also repudiated any suggestion that this was an opportunity for sensationalism and filth. Members had got beyond the sins of the flesh. Pride was their chief peril.[1] Together with this was simplicity, such as Charles Wesley noticed in the Welsh enthusiast, Howel Harris.[2]

But although John Wesley was even more concerned about what happened after conversion than in conversion itself, the real framework of Methodist piety even in the earliest days was that action of God upon the soul, which often violent and accompanied by strong crying and tears, brought a man from conviction of sin to assurance of

[1] *Letters*, III, 327.
[2] See G. F. Nuttall, *Howel Harris, the last enthusiast* (Cardiff 1965), p. 54.

faith; not what Wesley received through Jeremy Taylor, Thomas à Kempis and William Law, in 1725, but what occurred through pietistic influence in 1738. This was the beginning from which all other benefits flowed. It might take place in the open air, or in a little society, or at the very Table of the Lord. This gave the believer a new song, which helped at once to relieve his feelings, contain his emotions, perhaps to silence mobs, and unite him to the pilgrim company, 'the Church of pardoned sinners exulting in their Saviour'. This gave him entry to what Alexander Knox described as that 'cheerful piety, habitual pleasure in devotion and consequent settled self-enjoyment, which John Wesley maintained to be the inheritance of the true Christian'.[1]

[1] Alexander Knox, *Remains* (London 1834), IV, 282.

CHAPTER TWO

NINETEENTH-CENTURY MODIFICATIONS

THE scantiest survey of Methodism in the nineteenth century makes us aware that many of the distinctive characteristics of the earliest days remained, and that Wesley himself exercised remarkable posthumous influence in governing the devotional habits and the spiritual reading of his people for many generations.

What would Lopez and de Renty have thought had they known that their immortality would rest not simply on the fashionable salons of Paris or the parsonages of rural England, but on the diary references of broad-backed, stentorian, travelling preachers of the lower middle classes who laboured in the grime of an industrial civilization they could never have conceived? There was, for instance, a Wesleyan minister named Thomas Collins, who lived from 1810 to 1864, worked with intense evangelical ardour in many circuits from Orkney to Camborne, and not only read Lopez and de Renty but experienced something of their immediacy of communion with God. As a young minister in his twenties at Sandhurst, Collins wrote: 'I do in some measure give myself unto prayer; but O that I could feel that experience of Gregory Lopez mine: Every breath is prayer!' When he was dying, he devised a new almanack of devotion based on the three Persons of the Trinity, of whom, according to his biography, he had long, like the Marquis de Renty carried about 'an experimental verity'.[1]

1 Samuel Coley, *Life of Thomas Collins* (London 1869), see pp. 60, 485.

When he was asked about this, he replied 'I am in possession of no secret. I have never either looked for, or had, anything mystical, anything beyond what plain Scriptures warrant. I do not suppose that I have any divine manifestations peculiar to myself. The ordering of my thoughts in the manner I have told you of is not "of commandment"—is not the result of any extraordinary leading. It began as a mental choice; being found convenient and profitable, it has grown into a habit. In acts of devotion my mind sees its way most clearly when it talks with one Person. I, therefore, seeking edification, speak unto each of the ever-glorious Three distinctly in behalf of such things, and such things only, as Holy Scripture sets forth to be the province of each distinctly.'

In a prayer of Collins's last days, which follows, the three Persons are addressed each in turn, the Father as Strength and Joy, ever-beloved, to be glorified in death; the Son as the One who of old led his people through the Red Sea and will bear Collins safe through the waves of his departure from this world; the Spirit as the gift of Jesus, living and active in response to faith; the Triune God as omniscient Helper to whose will the soul must be resigned.[1] There is some danger of tritheism here, since Christian prayer is *to* the Father, *through* the Son, *in* the Holy Spirit, and the doctrine of the Trinity, vital to Christian Faith, is of personality *in* God rather than the personality *of* God.

Collins disclaimed 'mystical' experience, which he seems to regard as reserved for the spiritual aristocracy and dubiously scriptural. Yet more than once this man, who would sometimes spend Friday in 'secret fasting, meditation, and prayer for help on the Lord's Day', knew an immediacy of the Divine Presence which has some of

[1] Ibid., pp. 485 ff.

the marks of classic mysticism. On the Covenant Sunday of 1849, for instance, as, about five o'clock in the morning, he was preparing for the solemnities of the renewal, 'I was waiting upon God in believing acts. He mercifully drew near to me, as once—only once before—He did years ago, on the Rock of Skarfskerry. His coming darkened and distanced all earthly things. My soul felt as if within the cloud of Tabor. While it hung around me, I cried, "I know Thee! Yes, I know Thee!" The ineffable glory did not long abide, such specialities of manifestation never do; but in its gentle ascent it left a sweet life, a calm, a tenderness which cannot be expressed.'[1]

The darkness and the cloud, the ineffable glory, and the transcendency of the experience are typical of that Augustinian and Western Mysticism so brilliantly described by Abbot Cuthbert Butler.[2]

On Christmas Day, 1864, two days before his death, Collins repeated lines from Charles Wesley's hymn on the Crucified—*With glorious clouds encompassed round.*

> *Will He forsake His throne above,*
> *Himself to worms impart?*
> *Answer, thou Man of Grief and Love!*
> *And speak it to my heart.*

He died trusting in the blood of Jesus and healed by the stripes of the smitten Shepherd. He had always preached the Atoning Sacrifice. It was Thomas Collins who, when a Cornish butcher of wicked life cried out in agony of conscience, 'I am lost! I am lost! I have nothing!'; replied, 'Nothing? Why, man, *all the hill of Calvary belongs to you*!'

There is no more remarkable instance in nineteenth-century Methodism of the prayer of communion with

---

[1] Ibid., p. 291.
[2] Cuthbert Butler, *Western Mysticism* (1922 and 1926). Cf. p. 34 supra.

God than that imparted by the Primitive Methodist preacher John Nelson in his reminiscences of William Clowes (1780–1851) co-founder of his connexion. Clowes, be it noted, had undergone a disturbance of spirit prior to conversion when he recalled at a Methodist Love Feast a phrase from the Book of Common Prayer about taking the Sacrament unworthily, so that the Anglican Divines were his spiritual ancestors as truly as they were those of Methodism as a whole. But it was not echoes of the Prayer Book which impressed those who said of him 'We never heard prayer like this. . . . He lived and moved as though he were on the borders of the heavenly world.' During long and arduous missions in the north he would every now and then ask for an hour in which to pour out his soul to God, and he would do so without any agony, conflict or wrestling.

> . . . Sometimes when sojourning in the home of pious poverty, where there was not a second room where he could enter, he would say to the good woman of the house; 'Now I want to pray; pursue thy work; never mind me: and then without a word he would quietly kneel down in the most retired corner, where he could remain for an hour. Generally there was no audible expression . . . no sound heard. . . . There was an awful stillness. . . . He somehow in his solemn quiet sweetly sank into God, till he became motionless as a statue.[1]

The nineteenth-century missionaries, sent out by all branches of the by now fissiparous Methodism, testify in their journals to many experiences of immediate encounter with God, though perhaps the language of devotion becomes rather conventional, 'Was enabled last night to enter "the holiest of all" and hold communion sweet and rapturous with God' is a not untypical entry from a missionary's diary. There is much about 'the secret

[1] J. T. Wilkinson, *William Clowes. 1780–1851* (London 1951), pp. 85–6.

place'. Yet these men went out to the African fields in the knowledge that the climate and conditions might kill them in months, if not weeks. The toll of lives was appalling and those who remained were victims of often almost incessant fevers.[1] They were in many respects 'massively' heroic, counting all things loss for Christ. They do not seem to have had any doubts as to the truth of the Gospel they offered, and they died, often triumphantly, with Wesley's hymns on their lips, sure that they would be 'forever with the Lord'. They knew that they were supported by the societies at home—no account of Methodist devotion is complete without some reference to the great interest in missions overseas and the prayer which has sustained them. They knew also that behind their sacrificial efforts was the support of British civil and military power. But this did not deliver them from many hazards, and their secret is disclosed in the story of James Calvert, missionary to cannibals in Fiji who, once asked by a timid person, when he was on furlough, 'Were you not afraid of being killed?', replied, 'No, we died before we went.'[2] No textbook treatment of mortification can equal that!

We must now seek to survey as a whole the trends of Methodist spirituality during the nineteenth century.

THE DEVELOPING CHURCH-CONSCIOUSNESS

Though it was an age of world-wide expansion and great triumphs, the nineteenth century confronted Methodism with all the problems of continuing existence in the world; and, most notably, how to establish a durable Church

---

[1] Missionary work was perilous throughout the nineteenth century. See the story of the heroic United Methodist Free Churches' Missionaries to Africa and China in O. A. Beckerlegge, *The United Methodist Free Churches* (London 1957), pp. 89 f.

[2] Joseph Nettleton, *John Hunt* (London, undated but *c.* 1900), p. 27.

order and how to adapt itself to social changes. Some of
the problems were direct bequests from John Wesley
himself; his widespread sowing sprouted a harvest of
ambiguities and controversies as well as heroism, spirituality and intense faith.

For much of the century, Methodism lived in a love-
hate relationship to the established Church. It is difficult
not to feel that Methodism ought to have had such an
effect upon the Church of England as to make the later
Oxford Movement unnecessary. Why it failed is a very
complex matter; one very clear reason is that after the
Holy Club it had little or no influence in the universities,
and—snobbish as it sounds—movements of reform cannot
succeed without capturing the intelligentsia to a greater
extent than Methodism has ever done, at least in England.
(Its part in helping to create a West Indian, African and
American intelligentsia is another story.) But there is a
particular irony in the fact that, as has several times been
pointed out, it was early Methodist loyalty to the Church
of England, which at once destroyed the leavening power
it might have had and seriously impoverished its own
spiritual life.[1] Had not the Plan of Pacification (1795) been
so anxious to avoid the appearance of rivalry to the
established Church and refused to permit the celebration
of the Lord's Supper at church hours, the crowded
communions of the Wesleys, which made the revival
sacramental as well as evangelical, might have been a
feature of Methodism to the present day and made the
societies heralds of the liturgical movement.

At the same time, it must be recognized that this
judgement could be over-sanguine. The Sacramentalism
of the Methodist people in its hey-day was different from
that of the Catholic tradition—and the Puritan—and we

---

[1] See T. H. Barratt, *London Quarterly Review*, July 1923. Cf. J. C. Bowmer,
The Lord's Supper in Methodism, 1791–1960 (London 1961), p. 22.

must not allow our own quiet devotional reading of the hymns on the Lord's Supper to mislead us into a false idea of the atmosphere of eighteenth-century Methodist communion services. They were gospel feasts rather than holy mysteries, and the belief that the Supper was a 'converting ordinance' was a departure from the whole of Christian tradition even though *evangelical* conversion is implied, rather than a first turning from sin to God.

Nor must it be thought that the Sacraments meant nothing to nineteenth-century saints. Luke Tyerman told the story of *Praying William*.[1] This old man had a very serious attitude to baptism, and his Minister described a Communion service at which William was present, William began, as his custom was, to shout God's praises. but his voice faltered and his body shook. A sense of most sacred and solemn power filled the chapel. The Minister looked at William, 'his countenance lit up with joy and his body literally trembling', and thought of the words:

> *He visits now His house of clay*
> *He shakes His future home.*

The congregation rose, but William 'unconscious of any presence save that of Christ still kept kneeling and praising God'.

This is intense and genuine sacramental devotion but its differences from the Catholic tradition are perhaps as important as its similarities. Here is much more noise and 'enthusiasm', more obvious working up and psychological release. Christ possesses William rather than the bread and wine, which are not so much as mentioned; indeed the real presence is subjective rather than objective. 'The

[1] London 1857.

most sacred and solemn power' is in direct consequence of what happens to William not to the eucharistic species. William might, through a common love of Jesus, have understood that Breton peasant who, when he was asked why he spent so many hours on his knees before the reserved Sacrament, replied, 'I look at Him; He looks at me'. But he would not have been at home with the visual images or been able to direct his contemplation to the Sacrament itself. The darkened church, heavy with incense and *pietà* could not have been the context of his inspiration. He needed the bare chapel, probably bright in comparison, his fellow members of society around him, and the custom of vocal, noisy prayer.

From another branch of Methodism, Dr Beckerlegge has described the evening communion services of his youth, twentieth century in fact, but carried over from the nineteenth century.[1] Though it can be argued that it marks a departure from what Wesley would have approved, or from the way in which Methodism ought to have developed, this is in fact typical of most nineteenth-century practice. And before we deplore it as an impoverishment of what was or might have been it is well to recognize that it represented a genuinely intended fidelity to Christ's command and had a distinctive power, albeit different from Catholic sacramentalism, and not perhaps easy to recapture at the present time.

Certainly the differences from the Church of England began to be increasingly emphasized as the century wore on. The Oxford Movement despised and deplored Methodism, though it tried to recover the Eucharistic hymns.[2] Methodists, in their turn, were suspicious of what they felt were Romeward tendencies. The 1904

---

[1] O. A. Beckerlegge, *London Quarterly and Holborn Review*, October 1964.
[2] E.g. W. E. Dutton, *The Eucharistic Manuals of John and Charles Wesley* (London 1871). *John Wesley in Company with High Churchmen* (London 1869).

Wesleyan hymn-book amends the fourth verse of H. F. Lyte's *Praise my soul* to avoid the invocation of angels, and changes 'Son of Mary' to 'Son of David' in the funeral hymn *When our heads are bowed with woe.*

But even before the Oxford Movement, there were signs of a weakening of those Anglican ties, which in some ways had bound Wesley himself even more strongly after 1738. Thomas Jackson's edition of Wesley's works is comprehensive enough, but, for some unaccountable reason, he omits the Homilies of the Church of England, which Wesley had published at the very time when he discovered in his own experience the meaning of justification by faith alone.

There remained in Methodism a great love for the Book of Common Prayer. Adam Clarke would have no truck with Wesley's abridgement.[1] When the non-Wesleyan bodies began to devise their own service books they neither wished nor were able to break free of its hallowed forms. Some Methodists have read the daily Psalms in private and family devotion. But there has been also suspicion and dislike. The Islington Circuit sent a memorial to the Wesleyan Conference in 1874 urging that 'a revised and safe liturgy should be prepared and used instead of the Book of Common Prayer'. But this was after the Oxford Movement had poisoned relations, as was the complaint against the headmaster of a Wesleyan day-school in the Midlands, who used each morning in assembly the third collect for grace, 'O Lord and Heavenly Father, Almighty and Everlasting God who hast safely brought us to the beginning of this day . . .'.

There is little evidence that the Methodists of the nineteenth century were interested in Wesley's forms of prayer or in the Anglican tradition of ordered diurnal piety, Caroline and non-juring, which had meant so

---

[1] *Memoir of the Rev. Joseph Entwisle*, p. 239.

much to him. There was, however, a continual admiration of holiness wherever it was found. A Methodist preacher could write thus of the Jesuit founders, Ignatius Loyola and Francis Xavier: 'If the generality of that order have been deemed the most insidious of men, I think it equitable to avow my opinion that the founders of this institution were persons of deepest piety.'[1]

The violent and bitter controversies within nineteenth-century Methodism were all the result of attempts to resolve the ambiguities of Wesley's legacy. They were about government not spirituality. The authority of the Ministers was the nub of the contentions but the issue concerned political power rather than the lordship of faith, although there continued among the Wesleyans an antipathy towards lay administration of the sacraments, which caused a strong party to oppose Methodist union.[2] But there was little theological awareness on either side and Methodism has been, on the whole, innocent of the issues in disputes about orders and succession. It was ministerial rule which the non-Wesleyans so resented, for this was not the tyranny of a parish priest, powerful only within the limits of a defined area and checked by the existence of a slow-moving, not very efficient hierarchy. It was the claim by an exclusively ministerial conference to legislate for every society in the kingdom. The nineteenth century saw Methodism creaking and groaning into democracy, the non-Wesleyans by violent schism, the Wesleyans by gradual evolution.

It is easy to say that the separated and rival Methodists preached the same gospel, sang the same hymns and prayed with the same fervour, but internecine controversy cannot be good for a company of Christians who claim perfect

[1] Joseph Sutcliffe, *A Treatise on the Universal Spread of the Gospel, the Glorious Millennium and the Second Coming of Christ* (Doncaster 1798).

[2] See the opening essay in John Kent, *The Age of Disunity* (London 1966).

love as their grand depositum, and who inherit the sermon on the *Catholic Spirit*. But, apart from this, the whole transition from societies to church clearly resulted in a slackening of discipline, for while a society, like a religious order, consists of people of like mind, pledged to a rule of life, who may leave or be dismissed if they do not wish to obey, a church is inevitably a *corpus mixtum*, or, if you like, a dragnet which will bring in a curious and varied haul.

Throughout the nineteenth century, Methodism became increasingly unhappy about its failure to help its converts to grow in the Christian life. It has been said, apropos the Bible Christians, that both they and the Wesleyan Methodists, who spread side by side throughout North Devon in the fifty years after Waterloo, differed from the Prayer Book because they asserted that a personal Christian experience, rather than baptism, was the essential 'pre-condition of anything which can properly be called a Christian life'.[1]

But the records of Methodist history raise the question whether such personal experience is any more effective in ensuring that the believer endures to the end, or, less dramatically, makes real progress in the school of Christian love.

Numerous tracts were published urging the revival of real religion and the pressing on towards holiness. But in spite of the intensity of the few, there is little doubt that the many were always in danger of growing cold. Samuel Coley, theological Tutor at Headingley College, was forced to conclude 'Methodism has done much and well by *conquest*, but only little and inadequately by *nurture*'.[2]

[1] J. H. B. Andrews, 'The Rise of the Bible Christians', *Preacher's Quarterly*, March 1965, p. 58.
[2] S. Coley, *Life of Thomas Collins*, pp. 8-9.

REVIVALISM

In all this we may detect a shift of emphasis. It may be argued that throughout the nineteenth century and until the union of 1932, there was a crisis of identity in Methodism which produced a twofold tension. From 1795 there was no chance of Methodism becoming a Religious Order within the Anglican communion (though the latter phrase is an anachronism). The question was 'Is Methodism a Church and if so what kind of Church?', but in addition there was a haunting, half-embarrassed, half-conscience-stricken murmur 'Is Methodism a Church or a series of revivals?' The High Wesleyans, of whom Jabez Bunting was the much maligned representative leader, deplored the alternative, and were made uneasy by revivalists, whom they regarded as undisciplined and divisive.

There has been, and still is, a school of Christian thought not so far represented in the ecumenical movement, which would seem to regard Christianity as existing in this imperfect world by a dialectical process of revival—decline—revival. The Gospel is preached, many respond, but in time their religion becomes formal and lifeless, and so there is need for a new Pentecost.

> For several years, some of our members in different societies have appeared remarkably zealous in public worship, and have shown a disposition to assume the name of *Revivalists;* but a wish to preserve the union of the body induced us to check, with constant care, every distinction that in the least tended to a party spirit.[1]

In many Methodist Circuits and Societies of the nineteenth century, it seems to have been assumed that revival would be necessary every few years. The week's 'mission' became a feature of Methodist life, and although

[1] T. P. Bunting, *Life of Bunting*, Appendix K, quoted by H. B. Kendall, *A New History of Methodism* (1909), Vol. I, p. 556.

the hope was that this way local profligates and unbelievers would be brought in and converted (as indeed happened), there is little doubt that the main purpose of the preaching was to fan the flame within the lukewarm society. Of course, such missions were not the monopoly of Methodists or evangelicals in the nineteenth-century. They were a feature of Anglo- and Roman Catholic Church life, though, there, the emphasis may have been more exclusively on Calvary and less on Pentecost.

The greatest and most permanent revival within Methodism was that in the first decade of the century which began in those parts of north Staffordshire and south-east Cheshire dominated by the 'bleak and frowning summit' of Mow Cop. This is particularly relevant to our subject since it was so closely associated with prayer.

The 'prayer-meeting' was not a very common title in the eighteenth century, though John Wesley occasionally spoke with approval of it, and it is obvious that the bands and classes gave opportunities for free and spontaneous outpourings by members. Particularly was this so in the 'cottage-meetings' which by the end of the century had become characteristic of Methodist life in some regions of north-west industrial England. In north Staffordshire, these cottage-meetings, though 'lively and loud', were kept under strict control and limited to an hour and a half in time. This annoyed some who were denied the chance to express themselves in prayer and to these Daniel Shubotham, the cousin whom Hugh Bourne had converted, promised 'a whole day's praying on Mow some Sunday'.

It was not, however, until Bourne and his friends, who were already exercising an irregular revivalist ministry in the Potteries and north Staffordshire coalfield, were introduced to the strolling American evangelist, Lorenzo Dow, that the promise was fulfilled. Dow told them of the camp-meetings which had begun in America at the beginning of the century and were part of the technique of revivalism which was winning remarkable victories on the 'frontier'.[1] They were not confined to Methodism, but Asbury commended and encouraged them. They were, as a rule, typical scenes of religious enthusiasm, not without its attendant dangers. It is in some ways incongruous to think of the hymns of Isaac Watts, if not of the more rapturous Charles Wesley, being used to rouse their fervour; though as time went on, less poetic ditties were sung. At the Cane Ridge revival in Kentucky in 1801, Presbyterians, Baptists and Methodists were joined. The week-end of 6 August began formally enough, but by the Sunday there was an atmosphere of unearthly joy and many became 'convicted of sin'. One account noted that 'they say they feel very weak in their knees and a want of breath...' Ministers would then have the stricken carried out of the crowd and would converse, pray and exhort with each one. Others might sing an appropriate hymn. After a lapse of time the person might 'get comfort' through divine release and would exclaim, 'Lord, have mercy', then proceed to exhortations that onlookers cease doing evil, depend on Christ's righteousness, and in their turn seek the Lord. . . . Later stages were less restrained. Formal sermons seemed to give way, at least in part to small prayer circles of ten or twelve, each of which would sing a different Watts hymn, to be interrupted by a preacher mounting a stump or log to begin an informal discourse or fervent exhortation. One young man who attended later recalled that 'the noise was like the roar of Niagara', the people 'agitated as if by a storm'. He soon felt a peculiarly strange sensation. . . .' My heart beat

[1] For an account of camp-meetings see *The History of American Methodism* (1964), Vol. I, particularly pp. 507–23; also the many references to Lorenzo Dow.

tumultuously, my knees trembled, my lip quivered, and I felt as though I must fall to the ground.' Fleeing to the woods he returned to have the same experience again. 'My hair rose up on my head, my whole frame trembled, the blood ran cold in my veins, and I fled for the woods a second time, and wished I had staid at home.' Feeling almost suffocated and blind, he felt he would die; after a dismal night among the trees he set out for home, experiencing conversion the next day.[1]

The Methodists in England were suspicious of such uncontrolled excitement, which, so it was darkly hinted, fell easily into sensual excess; they had also been warned against Lorenzo Dow by an American leader who disapproved of his inveterate free-lancing and considered him a charlatan.[2] But Bourne, Clowes and Shubotham immediately saw that the camp-meeting could be an outlet and an extension of the enthusiasm which was engulfing the societies within the shadow of Mow. They also realized that held at the 'wakes' time, these assemblies could counteract the evils of the fairs.

There was a difference between those camp-meetings which were organs of the Primitive Methodist Connexion and their American prototypes. In a sense, the former were not *camp*-meetings, for each lasted but a day, albeit a long one. This, of itself, would be a safeguard against certain obvious perils.

At the first camp-meeting on Mow Cop there were four preaching stands constructed for the occasion out of pieces of rock, and each offer of the Gospel was supported by praying companies on other parts of the hill and beneath the wagonettes. Fervour, intensity and noise there was and singing of Wesley hymns but not the extremes of Cane

---

[1] *A History of American Methodism*, Vol. I, p. 513–14. The young man became a pioneer Methodist Minister in the Ohio valley.

[2] Ibid., p. 631.

Ridge. Indeed, Bourne seems to have been most impressed with the sight of 'thousands hearing with attention solemn as death', and modern writers of the Primitive Methodist tradition have stressed the centrality of prayer and the retreat to Mow Cop in order 'to seek comparative seclusion for a prolonged approach to God'.[1] And so, in time, a further Methodist Connexion was born. But our concern is not simply with the fervent, revivalist prayer of the camp-meetings, but also with the manifestation of a *lay* spirituality, spontaneous, of the people, and without sex distinction, which makes inevitable a comparison between Primitive Methodism and early Quakerism.

It was hardly to be expected that so acute a scholar as Dr G. F. Nuttall would read J. T. Wilkinson's biographies *Hugh Bourne* and *William Clowes*[2] without being stimulated to essay such a comparison.[3] Hugh Bourne had read Quaker books before his conversion and his desire for open-air worship was not derived from Lorenzo Dow so much as from the writings of the first Quakers. He visited the 'Quaker Methodists' of Warrington, whose cottage-meetings—detached and indeed outlawed by the Connexion—may well have been the inspiration of those with which he was connected in north Staffordshire. 'Here each one does that which is right in his own eyes. They stand, sit, kneel, pray, exhort, etc., as they are moved. I was very fond of their way.'[4] In their turn, some of the Quaker Methodists attended the camp-meetings on Mow Cop and Norton-le-Moors.

That Primitive Methodism did not find its spiritual

---

[1] Cf. N. H. Snaith, *The Methodist Recorder*, May 1957. W. E. Farndale, *The Secret of Mow Cop: A New Appraisal of the Origins of Primitive Methodism* (London 1950), p. 29.

[2] Published by Epworth Press in 1952 and 1951 respectively.

[3] Published in the *Friends' Quarterly*, to which this paragraph is indebted.

[4] J. T. Wilkinson, *Hugh Bourne*, p. 53.

home in union with the Society of Friends may be due to the fact that it was *early* rather than contemporary Quakerism with which Bourne had such affinities. By 1807, the Quakers were for the most part, a different social group from the industrial men and women along the course of the Trent whom the Primitive Methodists influenced. Again, Primitive Methodism (though this may be exaggerated) was something of a mass movement, which nineteenth-century Quakerism was not.

In *The Holy Spirit in Puritan Faith and Experience*, Dr Nuttall mentions two opposing views as to the relationship of Quakerism to Protestantism and Puritanism. Was it 'the fag-end of Reformation' or 'true Puritanism, purged of extraneous elements and carried to a conclusion not only logical but desirable'?[1] The same question may be raised about Primitive Methodism and its parent body. But it is not wise to stay for an answer, for we are dealing not with logic but with revivals, the movements of men's spirits which cannot be categorized and classified like butterflies in cases. All the same, there were very few who, once the first excitement was over, passed from Wesleyan to Primitive Methodism as to the logical end of their religious experience. Throughout the nineteenth century in all branches of Methodism, there was a perennial longing for revival, revival, and still more revival. On 9 September, 1848, Thomas Collins's father wrote to his son 'The present slow advance of Methodism becomes a grief to me. Surely our array—Ministers, local preachers, leaders, prayer leaders, sick visitors, tract distributors, teachers, ought to accomplish greater things. O for a baptism of the Holy Ghost! Bethesda was troubled before it could cure; and we must be better to do more. When fire infuseth its vehement heat, water seems all alive with motion. So when power from God thrills a church,

[1] Op. cit. (1947), pp. 13–14.

members and officers are full of holy zeal, penitents move, and the neighbourhood is stirred.'[1]

The manual which epitomized this longing and aided its satisfaction was. William Arthur's *The Tongue of Fire or the True Power of Christianity* first published in 1856. This went through eighteen editions in its first three years, and was still regarded as of sufficient importance to warrant a centenary edition in 1956.

Arthur was an Irishman whose life, from 1819–1901, was almost conterminous with that of Queen Victoria. He was loaned to the Wesleyan Missionary Society by the Irish Conference and had a short spell in Mysore, curtailed by an infection of the eyes. On his return, he was for most of his ministry a secretary of the Missionary Society, but he also served in several London Circuits, as Principal of the Methodist College at Belfast, and as President of the Conference. A serious weakness of the throat limited his preaching activities, but *The Tongue of Fire* is said to have begun as a sermon, which met with a similar reception to the famous lengthy utterance of the old Cambridge Puritan Laurence Chadderton, who, when he would have finished, was bidden 'For God's sake, sir, go on! Go on!'

Arthur's book is a study of Pentecost, which, though preserving a literalness and a historicity quite out of fashion today, is full of psychological understanding, keen imagination and apt analogy. He has the gift of entering closely into the hearts and minds of the followers of Jesus as they waited for Pentecost. How long the days after the Ascension must have seemed! Was the promise, after all, in vain? Whatever their distress and doubt they waited, and, (contrary to the besetting sin of revivalists and evangelists as Arthur knew it) they did not reproach one

---

[1] Samuel Coley, *Thomas Collins*, p. 285.

another, or probe too deeply into the cause of the delay by tortuous self-examination.

> John does not turn upon Peter and say, 'It is your fault; for you denied the Master'. Philip does not turn to John and say, 'It is your fault; for you and James wanted to lord it over us all'. Andrew does not turn to Thomas and say, 'It is your fault; for you *would* not believe, even when we had declared it to you'. The Seventy do not say, 'It is the fault of the twelve; for, after the Lord had lifted them above us all, one of them sold Him, another denied Him, and a third disbelieved'. The Marys do not say, 'It is the fault of the whole company, a cold and unfaithful company, professing to love the Master to His face, but the moment He fell into the hands of His enemies, ye all forsook Him and fled!' . . .
>
> Yet they knew He had not come to call the righteous but sinners, to repentance. . . . He knew every fault with which any of them could charge the others; yet the promise which had passed His lips, and the fire would fall on them unworthy as they were. Happy for them that none felt that he could fix on others the cause of their unanswered prayers.[1]

Indeed, Arthur's book is as clearly a corrective to the dangers of revivalism as it is a positive plea for hearts open to the power of the Holy Spirit. His Irish Protestant upbringing had given him an implacable hatred of Jesuistry, nor could he be expected to feel any tolerance towards Rome in the days of Pio Nono. But he is clearly a man of an evangelical *mean* in the controversy about set forms and extempore prayers, even though he insists that the Pentecostal gift is of spontaneous, unfettered prayer of the heart. This is what he says:

> Against such forms, suitably mingled with the public services of the Church we mean to say no word; we use, admire, and enjoy them; but, with the Acts of the Apostles open, it is impossible to repress astonishment that any man

[1] Op. cit., 1896 edn., pp. 18–19.

should imagine that frequent and formal reading of the best forms ever written, unmixed even by one outburst of spontaneous supplication from minister or people has any pretence to be looked on as the interceding grace, the gift of supplication bestowed upon the primitive Church. That in such modes holy and prayerful hearts may and do pour themselves out to God, we not only concede but would maintain against all who questioned it. That such prayers are in many ways preferable to the one set prayer of one dry man—long, stiff, and meagre—wherewith congregations are often visited, is too plain to need acknowledgement.

But gifts of prayer are part of the work and prerogative of the Holy Ghost. . . . In no form is the tongue of fire more impressive, more calculated to convince men that a power above nature is working, than when poor men, who could no more preach than they could fly, and could not suitably frame a paragraph on any secular topic, lift up a reverent voice amid a few fellow Christians, and in strains of earnest trust, perhaps of glorious emotion, and even of sublime conception as to things Divine, plead in prayer with their Redeemer.[1]

Arthur will not have it that the Pentecostal gift is the same as the glossolalia of 1 Corinthians 14 and other passages. It is rather a sign of 'a message from the Father of men to *all* men'. Thus he implicitly rebukes the extremists. Later, he declares that this is not one of the permanent gifts of Pentecost. Neither does he ignore the Sacraments.

On the day of Pentecost Christianity faced the world, a new religion and a poor one, without a history, without a priesthood, without a college, without a people and without a patron. She had only her two sacraments and her tongue of fire.[2]

[1] Op. cit., p. 90. For a remarkable story of the powers of prayer of a Durham miner, Isaac Hewitson, quoted from J. A. Findlay, see Leslie D. Weatherhead, *The Christian Agnostic* (London 1965), pp. 98–9.

[2] Op. cit., p. 65.

They continued steadfast 'in breaking of bread'; hence it is plain that it is not a purely spiritual system of worship, too spiritual to stoop to our Lord's ordained symbols or by the breaking of bread to show forth His death.[1]

William Arthur believes as strongly as Wesley that Christianity is a social religion, in two senses. The Church is the society of those who are each other's guides, philosophers and friends in the Christian life. He would probably have subscribed to the belief that outside the Church there is no salvation, provided it were understood that the Church is not primarily a hierarchic order, handed down from the first days, a supernatural aura surrounding its priests and rites; it is the fellowship of committed believers 'who kindly help each other on'. Nothing shows a more lamentable misunderstanding of evangelical Christianity than Father Hubert Northcott's assertion that 'John Bunyan's Christian had to leave home and kindred and set out on a lonely path. Here and there a companion joined him, but his pilgrimage remained a terribly solitary affair till he got to its end beyond the river.'[2]

William Arthur is nearer the truth; 'Banish from the Pilgrim's Progress the social element, the fellowship of hearts, the free recital of the Lord's dealings with each pilgrim, and you would cool its interest down to a point which, doubtless, would be decorous in the eyes of some, but would never touch the many.'[3]

Arthur also knows that Pentecost points to the 'general renewal of society':

The most dangerous perversion of the Gospel, viewed as affecting individuals, is, when it is looked upon as a salva-

[1] Op. cit., p. 91.
[2] Hubert Northcott, *The Venture of Prayer* (London 1962), p. 44.
[3] Op. cit., p. 97.

tion for the soul after it leaves the body, but no salvation from sin while here. The most dangerous perversion of it viewed as affecting the community, is when it is looked upon as a means of forming a holy community in the world to come but never in this.[1]

He is very much aware of the evils of society, but he has also stumbled on the paradox so powerfully expressed in our time by Reinhold Niebuhr—'moral man and immoral society'. 'Fearful social evils may co-exist with a state of society wherein many are holy, and all have a large amount of Christian light.'[2]

Arthur does not see the permanent benefits of Pentecost to the Church as portents or wonders, but as spiritual gifts and graces, communion with God, the victory of truth, the progress of the Divine life and grace among men, the joy and assurance of believers, the soul converting power of ministers. He looks forward with the optimism of grace and of a Victorian Englishman to the conversion of the whole world. But the secret is 'Remember the ten days'—'They continued with one accord in prayer and supplication.'

When a lecturer on electricity wants to show an example of a human body surcharged with his fire, he places a person on a stool with glass legs. The glass serves to isolate him from the earth, because it will not conduct the fire—the electric fluid: were it not for this, however much might be poured into his frame, it would be carried away by the earth; but, when thus isolated from it, he retains all that enters him. You see no fire, you hear no fire; but you are told that it is pouring into him. Presently you are challenged to the proof—asked to come near, and hold your hand close to his person: when you do so, a spark of fire shoots out towards you. If thou, then, wouldst have thy soul surcharged with the fire of God, so that those who come

<hr />

[1] Ibid., p. 87.   [2] Ibid.

nigh to thee shall feel some mysterious influence proceeding out from thee, thou must draw nigh to the source of that fire, to the throne of God and of the Lamb, and shut thyself out from the world—that cold world which so swiftly steals our fire away. Enter into thy closet, and shut to thy door, and there, isolated, 'before the throne', await the baptism; then the fire shall fill thee, and when thou comest forth, holy power will attend thee, and thou shalt labour, not in thine own strength, but 'with demonstration of the Spirit, and with power'.

As this is the only way for an individual to obtain spiritual power, so it is the only way for Churches. Prayer, prayer, all prayer—mighty, importunate, repeated, united prayer; the rich and the poor, the learned and the unlearned, the fathers and the children, the Pastors and the people, the gifted and the simple, all uniting to cry to God above, that He would come and affect them as in the days of the right hand of the Most High, and imbue them with the Spirit of Christ, and warm them, and kindle them, and make them as a flame of fire, and lay His right hand mightily on the sinners that surround them, and turn them in truth to Him. Such united and repeated supplications will assuredly accomplish their end, and 'the power of God' descending will make every such company as a band of giants refreshed with new wine.[1]

The dispassionate study of religious revivalism as a characteristic of nineteenth-century religious history is not yet available. The very moderation of the *Tongue of Fire* points to the difficulties of the Methodist position, Pentecostalist with a difference, convinced that the world must and will be won for Christ, theoretically organized to assist that sublime purpose, yet shy of extremes, aware of corybantic dangers and of the peculiar risk of charity being the first victim of evangelical fervour. In the second half of the century there were wings of Methodism

[1] Op. cit., pp. 195–6.

associated with movements very much peripheral to the great organized confessions, yet numerous and active.

The preaching of holiness was even more vigorous in America than in Great Britain. In his essay in *The History of American Methodism*, Timothy L. Smith describes the crusade in the twenty-five years before the outbreak of the Civil War. This owed much to a remarkable Methodist woman, Phoebe Palmer, a doctor's wife from New York City, authoress of innumerable tracts. It was, as Smith says, a concomitant of revivalism, of fervent preaching and mass conversions. Sinners were converted on an instant by the onrush of inexplicable, soul-tearing power; could not saints be similarly perfected? But Smith mentions other factors. 'The ethical ideals to which Emerson and Henry David Thoreau aspired on a highly sophisticated level, plain men of the time sought at a Methodist mourners bench or Class-meeting. Entire sanctification was a kind of evangelical transcendentalism which thrived amid the optimism the idealism and the moral earnestness which were so much a part of nineteenth-century American character.'[1]

The holiness movement was by no means indifferent to the social implications of the doctrine of perfect love. But it had its dangers. The idea of a 'second blessing', of perfection received in a moment, seriously upset the balance of Wesley's true teaching, which in its dependence on the spirituality of the great masters of the eastern and western Church, understands holiness much more in terms of the growth of an organism. In the metaphor of Macarius the Egyptian previously quoted, perfection is *not* 'Off with one coat and on with another'. Moreover, there was the likelihood that emotional excitement would be mistaken for ethical change and Mount Carmel obscure 1 Corinthians 13.

[1] Op. cit., Vol. II, p. 610.

In English Methodism, the Holiness Movement has had its centre in Cliff College. This was in fact founded by Thomas Champness, for the training of lay evangelists. He had previously opened a home for the purpose in Rochdale, and his intention was not only to give some book learning and practical guidance to men called to preach who would otherwise have had little chance of them, but also to provide a base from which Franciscan-style trekkers might go out on special tasks of evangelism. The College has in addition become the focus of a fervent and to some extent (though it owes much to its ordained tutors) *lay* spirituality. It has attracted those not altogether at ease in the respectable establishment Methodism of the connexional departments and the ministerial training colleges. In some ways very much a legacy of the nineteenth century and not without the dangers rife in that period of American Methodism, it has none the less, been the channel of a love of Christ, a sacrificial surrender to His claims and a zeal for the spread of the Gospel which otherwise could not have been contained in Methodism. It is from Cliff College that there have come those in the grand evangelical tradition of prayer, for whom talk of a 'minimum rule' of life would seem a response to the plenitude of grace so grudging as to be blasphemous. Who will nicely measure the minutes he will spend in the presence of Jesus Christ? Will not any time be too short for the incalculable joy of that conversation?

> *O the pure delight of a single hour*
> *That before thy throne I spend,*
> *When I kneel in prayer, and with Thee, my God,*
> *I commune as friend with friend.*[1]

From the biographies of nineteenth-century Methodists there emerges a pattern of Christian experience, which is

---

[1] Frances Jane van Alstyne (1820–1915), *M.H.B.* 746.

not peculiar to Methodism but was the common evangelical scheme. Granted that the home was Christian, the young child would be brought early to conviction of sin, often under the ministry of a revivalist preacher such as the Irish Gideon Ouseley, whose *Life* William Arthur wrote. There would be many tears, those infant cries and sobs which John Bunyan had felt were among the most blessed of all sounds. But, later on, in youth, there would be, as likely as not, a period of degeneration, a falling from grace, perhaps through a vicious school or wild companions, from which another revivalist was needed to bring recovery. After this, there was, often, no looking back. The Christian was committed to a life of service which would absorb every waking moment if he were a travelling preacher and all his leisure if he were not. Wesley's own full life was repeated in scores of his successors. And this intense dedication was nourished by a life of prayer. Wesley's own rule of early rising was encouraged by numerous exemplars, as indeed it was demanded by the conditions of rural and industrial labour. There would be Sunday morning prayer-meetings in the chapels at 6 or 7 o'clock, and, beforehand, the devout would be on their knees in private. 'Closet work', as it was somewhat quaintly called, was the duty and the joy of the true Methodist. After he had finished his working life, 'Praying William' would be upstairs at 11, 2 and 6 each day in obedience to Matthew 6[6], and doubtless also Daniel 6[10]. Often he would stump down exclaiming, 'O it has been precious! precious! precious! Bless Him! Bless Him!'[1]

This prayer was described also as heart-work in

---

[1] Luke Tyerman, *Praying William*. Cf. *Love and Life, The Story of J. Denholm Brash*, by his Son (London 1913), pp. 58 f., 'The Locked Study and the Open Heart': also R. N. Flew's address to the Pastoral session of the Methodist Conference 1946, *Methodist Recorder*, July, 1946.

language which could echo Richard Baxter's tribute to
George Herbert ('*Heart-work* and *heaven-work* make up
his books'). The periphrasis is eloquent of the passion and
love of Christ and men which inspired the prayer and
marked it off from all the tedious formalism of fussy
and overloaded schemes of devotion.

Fasting was practised both privately and by connexional
injunction, and there is no doubt that all those who were
serious about their religion obeyed without demur.

But the cry was always 'Revival'. On 28 January, 1843,
there was printed in Leeds *A Pastoral Letter on The Revival
of Religion Addressed Especially to the Wesleyan Methodists*.
It is this tract which speaks of 'heart-work', and appeals
for a theology of the heart in which truth will be seen
not as the test of orthodoxy and the weapon of controversy
but as the means of salvation and the rule of holy living.
Revivals, it is argued, are always necessary, because
'No human provision can be made against the secret
encroachment of a spirit of merely speculative inquiry'.

The main burden is a series of very practical counsels
to revive the Church, though it is asserted that 'our
beloved Connexion' is in no sense approaching a period
of decay. 'We have nothing to fear from outward opposi-
tion from any quarter, so long as we maintain the purity
of our doctrine, the vigour of our moral and religious
discipline, the possession and practice of real holiness
and the energy and simplicity of our zeal in seeking the
conversion of the world.'

These may be maintained as individual members
show a deep concern about religion, 'parents begin to
pray for and with their children', brothers and sisters,
masters and servants. The question should always be,
not 'How did you like the sermon?', but 'Did you profit by
it?' All the work of the Church should be supported and
cottage prayer-meetings attended, tracts distributed, and

help should be given with the religious instruction of the children of the poor. A resolve should be made to bring one additional person each quarter to class, one additional hearer to worship. The pledges of the Covenant Service are quoted.

Finally there is a Wesleyan insistence on the linking of prayer and faith with the *means* of grace, both instituted and prudential as Wesley, following Nelson, had distinguished them. Reading is included in the latter, particularly the lives of eminent ministers, such as Jonathan Edwards, and histories. One detects that in the Wesleyan body there was a certain disdain of what Augustine called 'the Sacraments of the humility of God's word'. Class-meetings and 'the good old-fashioned Church meetings our Lovefeasts' must not be neglected out of snobbishness. 'A fastidious taste may take offence at what is there spoken; but if so, the fact shows that the heart needs mending.' In all this Wesley, being dead yet speaks.

THE FAMILY

In no sense were the Methodists more the heirs of Puritanism than in their constant stress on the importance of family life and the household as the nursery of the Church. *A Plan of Scripture Readings for Family Worship* was published by Charles Atmore at Halifax in 1813. He writes with the confidence of approaching victory in the Napoleonic Wars. England will be saved by a praying remnant. He quotes the Puritan Oliver Heywood: 'When public persecutions break up Church assemblies family worship will maintain religion in the world. When ministers were banished (and he spoke feelingly being one of the banished ones himself) assemblies scattered, and churches demolished still the fire glowed hot on private hearths.'

There was much good advice as to the choice of marriage partners. 'If possible', writes Dr Walsh in his essay on

'Methodism at the End of the Eighteenth Century', 'Methodist married Methodist, remembering St Paul's injunction to the Corinthians: "be not unequally yoked with unbelievers".'[1] A hundred years later this was still the hope. One of my grandfather, William Henry Spooner's, manuscript addresses to his society class was given, so he notes, under the title of 'The Twelfth Commandment'; this is, according to him, another saying of St Paul, that marriage be 'Only in the Lord' (1 Corinthians 7[39]).

My grandfather's exegesis leaves much to be desired since Paul is in fact writing of the re-marriage of Christian widows (which he is inclined not to advise) and the chapter is concerned entirely with the situation of Christians in Corinth in the middle years of the first century and the problem of the mixed marriages of Christians and pagans. It is saturated with an eschatology very different from the Victorian. But Spooner makes his point with Scriptural and contemporary illustrations. To take an ungodly wife (or husband) is 'this sin of sins, this crime of crimes'. There is a vehement attack on the deceitfulness of men, who are far worse than women, including the very questionable statement indicative of the Victorian attitude to women in the age when make-up was reserved for theatricals, 'We don't often find young ladies attiring just to please their suitors, but men often put on a false exterior to deceive innocent girls'. There is a lurid concluding story of a Methodist Minister's daughter, who, against all advice, married an ungodly man. Before long she was made ill by her husband's cruelty, and the narrative passes into the present tense to recount the pitiful end. 'A broken-hearted father endeavours to point a wayward child to a deserted heavenly father and oh! the last words she utters they rend that father's heart and

[1] *A History of the Methodist Church in Great Britain*, p. 311.

how they make one shudder at their awful import—"I can't get over the gulf" she exclaims and dies.'

But, earlier, the class-leader quotes stanzas in imitation of Charles Wesley:

> *When e'er by noxious cares oppressed*
> *On the soft pillow of her breast*
> > *My aching head I'd lay*
> *At her sweet smile each care shall cease*
> *Her kiss infuse a balmy peace*
> > *And drive my fears away.*
>
> *Together would we meekly bend*
> *Together should our prayers ascend*
> > *To praise the Almighty's name*
> *And when I saw her kindling eye*
> *Beam upward to her native sky*
> > *My soul should catch the flame.*
>
> *Thus nothing should our hearts divide*
> *But on our years serenely glide*
> > *And all to love be given*
> *And when life's little scene was o'er*
> *We'd part to meet and part no more*
> > *But live and love in heaven.*

Family prayers were assumed as the framework of the Christian home. Methodism did not confine public religious services to the Lord's day; there was not quite the Puritan assumption that on the six days of labour the church was the house; Methodists used their chapels for mid-week meetings for prayer, class, preaching and revival. But it was expected that public worship and private prayer should be assisted by what was done in the family, which in its ideal was not so very different from what Burns describes in 'The Cotter's Saturday Night':

Then kneeling down to Heaven's Eternal King
The saint, the father and the husband prays:
Hope 'springs exulting on triumphant wing'
That thus they all shall meet in future days
No more to sigh, or shed the bitter tear,
Together hymning their Creator's praise,
In such society, yet still more dear;
While circling Time moves round in an eternal sphere.

'Praying William' once refused a holiday which some friends were willing to provide for him. 'No! no! I cannot go; for if I go, who will pray night and morning with my poor children.'

It was hoped and prayed that through the family influence children might early be won for Christ. I remember an octogenarian lady in my first Circuit in the mid-1940s who told me how her mother, a Yorkshire Primitive Methodist, a charwoman and very poor, would go each week to the chapel prayer-meeting and ask that her children 'might see the King in his beauty'. The pre-natal period was reckoned, in Aristotelian fashion, to be of supreme importance in shaping a child's character and destiny. Thomas Collins's biographer writes of the 'precious pre-consecration of life by maternal purpose and prayer'.[1]

My own mother never ceased to believe that I became a Minister because during her pregnancy she had been a class leader engaged in regular study and preparation which included the reading of Milton (perhaps with the half-conscious hope that I should be, not a Minister, but a man of letters?)

There was in nineteenth-century Methodism a tradition of the Christian child, dedicated, precocious and, like as not, sickly. The type owes its existence not simply

[1] Samuel Coley, *Thomas Collins*, p. 9.

to family religion but to the illness and mortality rate in the new industrial society whose *laissez-faire* system could not cope with its problems and where disease was not properly understood.

At Manchester there was first published in 1827 a little book destined to go through five editions.

EXAMPLES OF EARLY PIETY

Written for the Benefit of Children
and
Encouragement of Parents

Consisting of Memoirs
of
JAMES B. JONES
and a
Brief Notice of ELIZABETH E. JONES

By their Father

Mr Jones, Snr, was a Wesleyan Minister; neither of his children reached adolescence. The boy, James, was a solemn though loving child who once moved his father by embracing him with the words, 'I love you, papa, and I love God Almighty; and when I go to heaven I'll kiss Him too.'

Needless to say, the boy was delicate and one winter he and his sister were both very ill. The girl died, but James survived to endure an appalling erysipelas. His talk was mostly of heaven, though he admitted once that eternity was a subject that he could not comprehend and he was much puzzled by the thought of going on for ever. Yet on his birthday, as he lay watching his birthday cake being cut up for his friends (I opine mostly adults), he said, 'The day of my death will be better than the day of my birth. God loves me and has pardoned my sins.' He took time in her presence to express some doubts as to the spiritual state of a young woman who had come to visit him ('Miss S. is not quite *right*'), then he went on: 'Mine is an affecting case, but at the same time it is a glorious one. Who would have thought that God would be so kind to such a little boy as I am. I am happy! O I am very happy. I wish you would tell other little boys how good the Lord has been to me; perhaps it may do them good; perhaps they may also come to the Lord Jesus Christ and be happy also.'

He suggested that they sing a hymn; and they did, Charles Wesley's

> *O disclose Thy lovely face!*
> *Quicken all my drooping powers*
> *Gasps my fainting soul for grace*
> *As a thirsty land for showers;*
> *Haste, my Lord, no more delay*
> *Come, my Saviour, come away.*

with its echo of Augustine's *Confessions* in the second verse:

> *Well thou knowest I cannot rest*
> *Till I fully rest in Thee. . . .*[1]

A week or two later James B. Jones died. He was just nine.[2]

Sometimes the child would grow up but be stricken

[1] *M.H.B.* 545. This was not included in the edition published in John Wesley's lifetime.

[2] It is interesting to compare his record with that of W. R. Inge, the Dean of St. Paul's, almost a century later who in the chapter, *Bereavement* in *Personal Religion and the Life of Devotion* (London 1924) tells the story of his little girl Paula, who died aged 11, in 1923. Allow for the vast difference of culture between the two homes and the contrast between evangelical sentimentalism and loquacity, and Anglican Platonist restraint, and the two lives have more in common than either has with a modern pagan or Methodist child.

by consumption or cholera very early in manhood. Most
societies had their memories of such and often they were
renowned for the love of Jesus and for promise unfulfilled.
In his manuscript book, W. H. Spooner has copied some
verses by his brother, George, who died in the early
twenties. They are conventional enough and imperfect,
but interesting, since they come from 'the grass roots', and
state very simply the evangelical faith and hope of a
young man with but a short time to live. They show too
that the hymn-book tradition was still alive and it was
natural for Methodists, even the humble ones without
any particular genius, to express themselves in verse.

RETURNING TO JESUS

Jesus again I'll fly to Thee
And give my wanderings o'er;
For Thou hast died on Calvary,
And Thou my sin hast bore.

Now Lord receive Thy wand'ring child
Who far from thee has gone;
Come Jesus pityful and mild,
And claim me as Thine own.

Repentance, faith and pardon give
And also give me grace
And make me fit in heaven to live
Where I may see Thy face.

Now that I can my pardon claim
Through Jesus' painful death,
I'll always try to speak his fame,
As long as I have breath.

Some familiar Methodist notes are there; 'I'll praise my
Maker while I've breath', for instance, and the evangelical
conviction of sin and of wandering, but to be holy is to be

fit for heaven rather than to be made perfect in love. Heaven indeed was even more a preoccupation than in a century earlier, and if it comes to that, nineteenth-century preachers probably had more to say about hell than did Wesley.

The great cornerstone of family as it was of national religion was the observance of Sunday, called by the devout, the Sabbath. This again was Puritan and the doctrine propagated by Nicolas Bownde in 1595 that the Christian Sunday is virtually the same as the Jewish Sabbath went on its triumphant course in English Christianity.[1]

Stories were told of judgements on Sabbath breakers very reminiscent of Lewis Bayly's admonitory *exempla* in *The Practice of Piety* (1612) which, after all, was issued for the last time as late as 1842. A dissolute young man, for instance, might be brought to a sense of sin through a storm buffeting the boat in which he had sailed to illicit Sabbath pleasures.

> *The gay who rest nor worship prize*
> *Jehovah's changeless sign despise*
> *May we the worth of Sabbaths learn*
> *Before we suffer in our turn.*

So wrote William Maclardie Bunting, son of Jabez, in a hymn which survived until 1933. (He did write better hymns than this, such as 'Blessed are the pure in heart', though even here there is a Sabbatarian verse.) In the library of the Leys School at Cambridge there are still works classified as 'suitable for reading on Sunday' by the *imprimatur* of the last clerical headmaster, who retired in 1934.

---

[1] Nicolas Bownde, *The True Doctrine of the Sabbath; before and under the Law, and in the time of the Gospell* (enlarged edition London 1604), cf. C. J. Stranks, *Anglican Devotion* (London 1961, p. 49).

The Methodist Victorian Sabbath does not need defence. The technological revolution bids fair to obliterate what the industrial revolution largely spared, but for the Methodist working men of last century, Sunday was at once the beginning and the crown of the week. 'Now we have done with the world till Monday morning', Lax of Poplar's father would cry as he finished work on Saturday. Before rest there would be preparation for Sunday. Shoes were cleaned and food prepared so that all unnecessary duties could be avoided on the Lord's Day. John Newton's Olney hymn for Saturday evening was sometimes sung, certainly by the women students of Southlands College in the 1880s:

> *Safely through another week*
> *God hath brought us on our way,*
> *Let us now a blessing seek*
> *On the approaching Sabbath day,*
> *Day of all the week the best*
> *Emblem of eternal rest.*

Rest or no, the Sabbath was a long day for the Society leader or local preacher, or for the 'enquirer' (the equivalent perhaps of the catechumen). 'Praying William' had been drunken and profligate in his youth and he was first turned to serious thoughts by going to visit a sick friend and having a conversation about heaven. This and the solemnities of the subsequent funeral drove him to spend Sunday with the Methodists at Norfolk Street Chapel, Sheffield. This meant that on that first occasion he heard three sermons and attended the prayer-meetings, beginning at 6 a.m. But since he believed that his eternal destiny was at stake he could hardly grudge the time or complain that the sermons were too long. Later on, the Methodists whose Sundays were crowded with services and Sabbath school and organization would sing lines by one of their famed preachers, William Morley Punshon (1825–81):

At work for God in loved employ
We lose the duty in the joy.

This was true to experience in the more prosperous, neo-Gothic churches at the end of the century; among the Methodists of the proletariat, depressed in the middle years, Sunday was a day when the working man was given a place and a voice and made aware of his dignity as a child of God.

A PIETY BASED ON PREACHING

The last fifty years of the nineteenth century was the era of great preachers, and Methodist spirituality was undoubtedly influenced by the cult of the pulpit. This was to some extent a departure from the distinctive Methodist norm, which had conceived of the preacher chiefly as evangelist, often in the open air, and had relied on class meetings more than sermons for the schooling of saints. Thomas Collins' biographer treats himself to one of his lengthy improving asides on this theme:

' "Methodist Preachers!"—the designation suggests our lack while it expresses our power. People say that "we preach well". If practice can insure that, we certainly ought to do so. The inexorable pulpit demands of Methodism are more numerous than those of any Church in Christendom; but is preaching everything? . . . But venerable and honourable as is their appellation (Methodist Preachers) it is neither older nor better than "Pastors and teachers" of Eph. IV, 11. . . . The lambs will never be fed by a mere sermon mill. Hooker says "The delivery of elements should be framed to the slender capacity of beginners". They must be catechised.'[1]

[1] Samuel Coley, *Thomas Collins*, pp. 95–6.

In *The Tongue of Fire*, William Arthur contrasts the convention of his own time with the religion of Pentecost, which made all Christians witnesses. 'Let them ask if it is like their religion that one lonely minister shall, on the Lord's day, bear witness before a thousand Christians, who decorously hear his testimony as worthy of acceptance by all, and then go away and never repeat the strain in any human ear?

'Looking on the universal movement of that Pentecostal day who will think that the new religion was ever to come down to this, that speaking of its joys, its hopes, its pardon, its mercy for the wide world was to be considered a professional work for set solemnities alone, and not be a daily joy and heart's ease to ever growing multitudes of happy simple men?'[1]

Be that as it may, by the end of the century, Methodism was little distinguishable from the other Free Churches, as they were now to be called, in the belief that the strength of Christianity was to be measured by the large congregation hanging on the words of a preacher, whose sermons were less 'patient and formal expositions' than 'red-hot exhortation and dramatic religious demagogy.'[2] There was some attempt, as Routley has said, 'to reproduce under cover of a roof the open-air evangelism of the Wesleys' and the massed congregations of the Methodists, especially in the new Central Halls, were likely to include a much larger proportion of artisans and poorer people than those of the other Free Churches.

The effect on the spiritual life and its patterns was considerable. On the face of it a popular sermon may not seem a very good medium for spiritual direction, and certainly the modern fashion is to despise it in the name of sound educational method (which I, in turn, am

[1] Op. cit., p. 56.
[2] Cf. Erik Routley, *English Religious Dissent* (Cambridge 1960, pp. 168 ff.).

inclined to suspect as a synonym for the latest fad of our pedagogic conditioners). But the sermon has a long history as a primary means of instruction[1] and those who went to Central Halls on Sunday nights or suburban churches on Sunday mornings may well have received understanding of the Gospel and help in Christian living through the sermon which 'group dynamics' would not have given them. For one thing it may not be physically possible to organize a thousand people in classes; for another, there are many who do not respond to group methods, who may learn something from a sermon. The danger is that 'rostrum Christianity' may be wanton, heretical or narrow. Great problems may be brushed aside by a few cheap illustrations or rhetorical phrases, public taste rather than truth may dictate what is said, and the preacher, governed by the desire to find favour and maintain crowds may be led into an utter loss of integrity. The desire to give people a secure and strong faith and never to undermine their confidence that 'God's in his heaven all's right with the world' is in many ways admirable but breeds distrust in the next generation. Alternatively, the abstract denunciation of social evils without a genuine and sympathetic understanding of their cause or knowledge of their cure is an inveterate danger whether those evils be drink, prostitution, segregation or war. More and more the distance between the sermon and the life of the world increases, and going to church becomes an activity of the twilight, or a dream which dies at the opening day. A pulpit style and language are handed down which, though less ugly than the jargon of our scientific culture and no harder to understand in themselves, sound hollow, meaningless, irrelevant and

[1] Cf. H. R. McAdoo, *The Structure of Caroline Moral Theology* (London 1949), p. 12, et seq., 'The general medium of moral theology for Anglicans will be the sermon.'

ineffective, appropriate prey for *Beyond the Fringe*. A church whose chief intellectual activity is preaching will substitute declamation for argument, and perorations for scholarship.

Yet since our task is to interpret, not simply to criticize, we must recognize that the increasing belief that the principal religious act of the week was the hearing of a preacher gave to Methodist spirituality a pattern of its own with which the other Free Churches were not so deeply stamped, since preaching for them was not to the same extent shared by laymen.

After all, a sermon is a form of meditation and the assembled congregations were really being taught this technique without knowing it. Perhaps the connection was not always made plain, but in fact if the hearer had applied the method of the Sunday sermon to his own private reading of the Scriptures he would have been engaged in a classic Catholic activity of the spiritual life. If he had completed his exercise with a Wesley hymn he might have been brought to the verge of contemplation. What is more, 'a Methodist layman may spend much of his leisure time preparing a sermon or Sunday school lesson or thinking what he is to say to his class; he may never think about the methods of meditation; but he sits with his Bible or his Hymn-book in his hand actually meditating'.[1]

The piety of the sermon meant that the Methodist images were mental and verbal, not visual. The chapels of the later Victorian era were more 'decorated' than those of the earlier period, but there was a reluctance to co-ordinate church design with worship. It was by no means assumed that an Anglican type building would mean a Prayer Book service; indeed the buildings, as with the

[1] A. Raymond George, 'Private Devotion in the Methodist Tradition', *Studia Liurgia*, Volume II, No. 3, September, 1963, p. 233.

other Free Churches, were first and foremost status symbols. Crosses and simple ceremonial crept in very gradually to public worship, to a large extent after 1945, and for some decades there were Methodists who would encourage in the Sunday school what they abominated in church. This was not detestable inconsistency; rather a Puritan belief that the full-grown man in Christ should have put away childish things. The Methodist eschewed visual aids in worship for the same reason that he closed his eyes in prayer; he would have found them distracting. The wonder of the Gospel ought to be enough in itself to require no ornament. This did mean that the good Methodist was used to concentrating his mind on the sermon and thinking the preacher's thoughts with him, not always in a mood of submissive acquiescence. Listening to sermons whetted the critical faculties, though often a judgement of content was in fact a judgement of the preacher's personality. The pre-eminence of the sermon could make the rest of the service but preliminaries and it led to a failure to understand liturgy as well as a tyranny of words. He is a rarefied, fastidious and perhaps 'unco-guid' Methodist who really appreciates silence. And in the nineteenth century at any rate it was what he *heard* that moved him and brought him into the presence of God.

CHEERFULNESS BREAKING-IN

The Methodist life in the nineteenth century was narrow by twentieth-century standards, as it was bound to be until the Church could be fertilized by the universities. The Education Act of 1871 has over the years transformed English dissent; perhaps it has killed it. John Kent has written of the historical autonomy of Methodism in the 1850s: 'It contained thousands of people for whom life was a Wesleyan creation, who saw the surrounding world through Wesleyan spectacles, for whom the future of

Wesleyan Methodism mattered far more than the fate of secular empires far away in a different dimension.'[1] Any other Methodist name could be substituted for Wesleyan. By the end of the century, Methodists were becoming more concerned in the wider political and social issues of the world, but in 1890 Richard Green, though convinced that Methodism would always be needed, had to admit that it 'may not be adapted to meet the preferences of the people of the country generally. . . . It may lack the necessary comprehensiveness'.[2]

There is something majestic about late Victorian Methodist piety even in its narrowness. A friend has told me how, as a boy, he was once staying in the home of his grandfather, a Methodist Minister, and a vivacious young aunt bought a pack of playing cards and was teaching him to play. When the grandfather discovered them at their game, he not only delivered a stern and sorrowful reproof, but retired to his study and spent two hours wrestling in prayer for their salvation.

At the same time, the life of the Methodist people was not completely circumscribed by work and chapel. Nature interested them and many became students of flowers, trees, birds and butterflies. The study of the Bible itself led them to history, archaeology and languages. My grandfather talked to his class about the manners and customs of the ancient Egyptians as well as about saving faith, about scientists and the speed of light, as well as unconditional election, while, preserved in his manuscript book itself, are some threads of glass fibre. W. H. Dallinger, a Wesleyan Minister who died in 1909, was a Fellow of the Royal Society, and a household word among the better informed older Wesleyans of my boyhood. From 1888 he

[1] John Kent, *The Age of Disunity* (London 1966), p. 102.
[2] Richard Green, quoted by Henry D. Rack, *The Future of John Wesley's Methodism* (London 1965), pp. 37–8.

was set apart by Conference to develop his work on the 'biology of micro-organisms'. As late as 1940, I heard him cited in a sermon as having demonstrated beyond all doubt that 'all life was life derived'.[1]

Methodists became interested in sport and were to take their share in the new world of mass entertainment in the twentieth century. John Denholm Brash (1841–1912), whom both R. N. Flew and W. E. Sangster instance as an example of Christian Perfection, was debating the selection of the England Test Team in his last illness a few days before his death. 'He would speak about Christ and cricket in the same breath, and about cricket averages and the missionary problem.' He was also interested in football, athletics and golf.[2]

The characteristic note of Methodism was still cheerfulness. The *Class Leader's Assistant*, published in 1857, declares that Christians must not hang down their heads or have quivering lips. They must rejoice in their religion, and this they will do because a good conscience gives them the assurance of the favour of God and an interest in heaven. The manual goes on to quote a recent hymn (1847) by Mary Peters (*née* Bowley). She was in fact an Anglican married to a Gloucestershire incumbent, but it is interesting and appropriate that Methodists should find it congenial, for inartistic jingle as it is, it echoes directly Julian of Norwich:

> *Through the love of God our Saviour,*
>   *All will be well;*
> *Free and changeless is his favour,*
>   *All, all is well:*

[1] For an interesting paragraph and footnote on Dallinger see Rack, op. cit., p. 33; also J. F. C. Dakin, *Methodist Magazine*, January 1966.

[2] *Love and Life, The Story of J. Denholm Brash*, by his Son, Ch. VI, 'The Sportsman'.

Precious is the blood that healed us;
Perfect is the grace that sealed us;
Strong the hand stretched forth to shield us,
    All must be well.[1]

This joy and confidence was based on a desperate conscientiousness; it could be stern. An early lesson for each child was that 'to obey is best' and more than one Victorian Methodist mother would have endorsed Susannah Wesley's words about 'breaking the child's will'. Yet the reward of goodness was presented as a happiness beyond this world altogether, which amid all the vicissitudes of life would never fail since its source was unclouded communion with the Saviour. No more than Wesley did Methodists indulge the belief that the Christian might need to pass through a 'wilderness state' of doubt and dereliction. I myself knew a Northumbrian miner, and a true saint if ever there was one, who always refused to sing William Cowper's lines:

Where is the blessedness I knew
When first I saw the Lord?

because he did not believe that if a Christian was faithful his joy in Christ would ever diminish, or the vision be clouded. This was undoubtedly his own experience and it was authentically Methodist, but too exceptional to formulate as a universal law of the spiritual life, as the *Class Leader's Assistant* itself implies when it gives some good advice to foster the believers' rejoicing. Answers to prayer must be looked for, the means of grace used, our own weakness of character discerned, prayer for one another in the Society constantly maintained, the longing for heaven kindled. This is classical, and shows that, in practice, the Methodists' belief that holiness is happiness

[1] *M.H.B.* 525.

did not make them naïve, or blunt the edge of their spiritual counsel. But the 'terrible twentieth century', with its moral and scientific earthquakes, was not only going to break down the old safe fences of religion and culture, but also leave a *malaise* and a desolation with which the simple piety of Christian joy would not easily cope.

CHAPTER THREE

TWENTIETH-CENTURY TRIALS AND HOPES

By 1914, the class-meeting was no longer the spiritual power that it had been in Methodism. Church programmes, in the ostensible interests of evangelism, had become filled with less intensive, more alluring activities. Rightly or wrongly there was some confusion of aim. Was Methodism primarily to enable men and women to help each other to fit themselves for eternal life, to pursue serious Christianity without relenting, to explore together the heights and depths of holiness, or was it to provide companionship, enjoyment and interest, to be a Christian alternative to the public-house and the social club, where people of all ages and both sexes might find recreation with temperance? Forty years earlier, as my grandfather's notebook shows, the class had become more than the Methodist equivalent of the confessional ranging little beyond the narrow way of Christian pilgrimage. Many meetings for testimony and the sharing of Christian experience remained, Love feasts were still planned, but the groups from which the young men went to war were mostly Pleasant Sunday Afternoons, or large 'fellowships' with hymn singing, Scripture and an address, little different in shape from worship in the congregation.

Classes or no, the first half of the twentieth century was the great age of groups, in which Christians banded themselves together to pursue common aims. It was out of such groups that the ecumenical movement sprang, though many of them were not inter-confessional. The pattern of activity was usually the same—a simple rule of life, perhaps, local meetings with a winter course of study, and always the annual Conference at High Leigh or Swanwick. The war, and the desire to maintain its camaraderie gave impetus to this movement, but in no sense created it, for many of the groups had begun before 1914.

The three most influential movements of this kind in Methodism were the School of Fellowship held annually at Swanwick, the Fellowship of the Kingdom for ministers, founded after the First World War, and, in the late 1920s and early '30s, the Cambridge Groups, the precursors of the University Methodist Societies, which were to go on gaining in strength for the next thirty years.

Certain eminent Methodist teachers were influential in all three, and we may gain most understanding of their contribution to the spiritual life, if we consider the work of W. R. Maltby, J. Alexander Findlay, R. Newton Flew, and the young Leslie Weatherhead. These four were variously associated, particularly at Swanwick, and, in the 1920s, influenced each other. They would have been the first to acknowledge their indebtedness to many other gifted men and women, ordained and lay, but theirs are perhaps the outstanding names. Maltby and Findlay were the most original, Flew was the most erudite and the most 'Catholic', destined to become an ecumenical theologian, while Weatherhead's amazing popular gifts advanced his fame far beyond the circle of students and disciples.

The spirituality of these four was based on the historical Jesus as he is described in the Synoptic Gospels. The purpose of a series of studies in *St Mark*, published as Manuals of Fellowship over more than a decade, but not extending beyond Chapter 6, was to help the members of the group to 'be present as if in the body, at every recorded event in the history of the Redeemer'.[1] To this task,

[1] John Ruskin, *Frondes Agrestes*.

the team brought scholarly gifts of translation and paraphrase (apart from the Gospels, Maltby's paraphrase of Romans 8 is masterly). They believed that each detail of the narrative, rightly understood, could make vivid the events in Palestine long ago, and help us to see Jesus as a real Person, while 'the manhood of Jesus, steadfastly contemplated becomes a vista into the nature of God'.[1]

Behind all this, there is an attempt to turn the devastating consequences of Higher Criticism to the service of faith. Great Methodist scholars like J. H. Moulton and A. S. Peake were also dedicated to this task. But some indication of the crisis of the times and the *malaise* of the ministry in the second decade of the century is given in these notes by R. N. Flew of a meeting held on 11 December, 1917.

> The Group met for the promised conversation on the actual state of our own religious experience. Seven men were there. . . . B. H. opened by a confession of his finding and losing. Christ was real for him for some weeks, but again he had lost the sense of the Presence. M. had come almost in despair. C. found something last February, owing to the reading of Burroughs, which he had never lost. I spoke of the state of my life since August.
>
> At the end M. asked us to pray for his old Father who is in a state of darkness, almost of despair.
>
> If we are a typical set of young preachers and if the occasion was not unfortunate, then there must be hundreds who are hungry for the rich experience of Christ. But when we are frank enough to unveil our own hearts we certainly do not seem victorious. But it is something that we can be so open. It is seldom that men can thus deliberately tell the exact truth to one another of the present state of their religious life.

[1] T. R. and W. R. Maltby, *Studies in St Mark* (i) (London, undated). Perhaps the apogee of this type of interpretation is seen in Weatherhead's ingenious psychological exegesis of the story of the Gadarene demoniac in both *It Happened in Palestine* (London 1936) and *Psychology, Religion and Healing* (London 1952).

The next day, Flew was at Westminster, at a meeting of his seniors, which seemed to be devoted to trying to decide whether or not men who regarded the early chapters of Genesis as myths were within the Methodist standards and should remain in the ministry. It was disappointingly inconclusive and Scott Lidgett was exasperatingly ambivalent, but Maltby 'prayed with strange intimacy and power'.

The *Studies in St Mark* are innocent of Form Criticism, the technique by which each section of the Gospels is studied as though its shape were determined, not by the report of an eyewitness or the art of a biographer, but by the preaching and mission of the early Church. To compare the Swanwick manuals with the *Study Outline on St Mark's Gospel*, which Alan Richardson prepared for the S.C.M. in 1940, or with Davis McCaughey's *Seven Studies in the Gospel according to St Mark* (S.C.M. 1951), is to notice a great change of emphasis. By 1940 Rawlinson and R. H. Lightfoot and their continental counterparts are in control. A new attitude to history and its limitations is in evidence. Richardson does recommend Findlay's *Daily Readings on Mark's Gospel* as a devotional accompaniment to his own pamphlet which has a more theological purpose. His Jesus shocks, and he and those he represents are not so ready to explain hard sayings away.

When Richardson and McCaughey come to the Parable of the Sower, they are concerned either with its teaching about the Kingdom of God, or its relevance to the situation of the first Christians, persecuted and liable to discouragement. They have neither the space nor the inclination for paragraphs like these of Maltby's:

> Even in the imperfect reports which have come down to us of the sayings of Jesus there are scattered words which betray a tender intimacy with growing things and country life. Pure in heart from His youth, He had looked on Nature

with understanding eyes. We owe much to the mystics on whom, through the visible works of God, His eternal glory breaks; but all their knowledge is as a drop in the ocean compared with the wealth of teaching which Jesus drew from the world around Him. And it would seem that at the time of which we are thinking the analogies of growing seed were much in His mind. Some of His followers were thinking that if they only had the power for twenty-four hours, they would fetch the Kingdom in. They had dreams of a national rising, of victorious armies and scattered enemies. Others looked to see the heavens opened, and the Son of Man coming in the clouds, an end of all debate. Always the same delusion, that force, if there is enough of it will do the deed! Jesus looks elsewhere for His similitudes. The Son can do nothing but what He sees the Father doing, and the Father's handiwork is all around Him. The parable of the seed growing secretly in the earth that bringeth forth fruit of itself, is conceived with a poet's insight, and it came from a heart full of faith, patience, humility, and quiet serenity.

Jesus was a tireless Sower, and He always sowed for a harvest. But He knew the harvest He sought could not be forced. Therefore He would neither coerce men nor nag at them. He knew how to sow His seed, and how to leave it alone. The message must be left to do its own wooing and the heart to make its own reply. The hireling finds it easy to 'leave it alone', but that is because He is not eager for the harvest, and knows not whether he has sown husks or seed. But Jesus spared Himself nothing in His sowing, and already much of the ground proved unfruitful. It gives us pause to see Him stand back to give room and time for the seed to grow, and to hear Him speak of the earth bringing forth fruit of itself, the sower 'knows not how'. There is such faith and humility in that word as might well bring the tears to our eyes. He knew indeed that He was not leaving the seed alone. He was leaving it to a thousand ministries, 'a mighty sum Of things for ever speaking', to the nature of men made for God, to the Spirit who never leaves us and the Love that will not let us go. The most sensitive and vulnerable heart that ever beat on earth was also the most serene. That is the miracle of Jesus. 'He sowed His seed over hill and dale, and on the last bare hill He sowed Himself.'[1]

This was then a company of friends, who may almost be said to have been a 'school' of meditation on the Gospels. The hymn, which could well have been their favourite, and which certainly epitomized their spirituality was Charles Wesley's:

> Open, Lord, my inward ear,
>   And bid my heart rejoice;
> Bid my quiet spirit hear
>   Thy comfortable voice;
> Never in the whirlwind found,
>   Or where earthquakes rock the place,
> Still and silent is the sound,
>   The whisper of Thy grace.
>
> From the world of sin, and noise,
>   And hurry I withdraw;
> For the small and inward voice
>   I wait with humble awe;
> Silent am I now and still,
>   Dare not in Thy presence move;
> To my waiting soul reveal
>   The secret of Thy love.
>
> Thou didst undertake for me,
>   For me to death wast sold;
> Wisdom in a mystery
>   Of bleeding love unfold;
> Teach the lesson of Thy Cross,
>   Let me die with Thee to reign;
> All things let me count but loss,
>   So I may Thee regain.[2]

[1] T. R. and W. R. Maltby, *Studies in St Mark* (iii) (London, undated), pp. 14–15.   [2] *M.H.B.* 465.

Leslie Weatherhead has been a considerable composer of prayers, and his card, *Ten Minutes a Day*, first printed in 1936, has gone through countless editions and must have helped many thousands of ordinary people to understand that prayer is far more than asking. As a preacher, he has always given as much attention to the conduct of worship as to the sermon.

Some would maintain that the true note of 'revivalism' is not heard from this group, which is of a different *genre* from the noisy Methodism, which would for ever shout 'glory', though it would not disclaim that parentage. But, on 4 October, 1915, Newton Flew wrote from his first church to his mother, deploring the action of one of his colleagues at a ministerial convention. The man had spoken,

> not without sense on entire sanctification. But he ends up by asking all who want to claim the blessing straight away to come out and line up in front, takes the meeting out of the Super's hands, lines up himself, dragoons two or three hoary saints out of their seats . . ., two or three trembling girls and has a high old time procuring the second blessing for these lined-up sinners. God forgive me but I do not like this way and fall into profanity when I think about it. Were Peter and John and the rest lined up in front on the day of Pentecost? Was our founder . . . lined up in Aldersgate Street? . . . Must I verily line up if I want to see the Lord? Ah, no, verily but it is hard for those of us who love Him in sincerity and passion to see misguided fanatics come along, torture sensitive hearts, spoil meetings aflame with desire, and try to force every experience on to the Procrustean bed of their narrow holiness.
>
> When will these fellows learn something of the awe, the tenderness, the delicacy, the mysterious issues which belong to the ministry of souls?

Years later, Findlay felt that the values of Methodism at the time of Union were not those of Jesus Christ.

We hear continually of the resources of our Church; He said that the richer you grow, the harder it is to get into the Kingdom.

The first question asked about a minister is, 'Is he an acceptable preacher?' He took it as an axiom that no prophet is acceptable among His own people, and at the end of three years ministry He was crucified by those to whom He came! We believe—or it would appear that we do—in advertising: 'He would not strive or cry', and seems to have been chiefly anxious that those who saw his wonderful works should not make them known. I know that such contrasts can be in various ways mitigated; is it not better to confess that on these matters we have not the mind of Christ?[1]

Maltby, Findlay and Flew were all anxious to make less ruthless than it had been the old dichotomy between sacred and secular. Grace was not to be the cuckoo which drove all other birds out of the nest! In *The Significance of Jesus*, first published in 1948, Maltby criticizes Jeremy Taylor's *Holy Living*, because it laments the time we must spend 'in eating and drinking, in necessary business and unnecessary vanities, in wordly civilities and less useful circumstance, in the learning arts and sciences, languages or trades'. Taylor does not help us to see that 'the appointments of this earthly life . . . are of God, and therefore have love and have friendly significance in themselves'.

So someone has said: 'If I am in the cotton business and feel the zest of it, does God feel any interest like my own? If I struggle with my picture and at last get my bit of cloud just right, does God care about that too? I enjoy *Punch* and *Pickwick*. Does God allow me to read them only as a sort of concession to my foolishness? If I mind a machine all day, does God care about my bit of skill, my accuracy and deftness? If I make buttons, does God care about buttons?

[1] J. A. Findlay, *Jesus the Perfect Man*, Sheffield Congress Booklets No. 6 (London, undated), p. 4.

If the little boys play football, does God only say, "Little things please little minds"?'[1]

It is from an article by Maltby in the *Methodist Recorder* of December, 1916, that Flew quotes to conclude his chapter on Methodism in *The Idea of Perfection in Christian Theology* (1934). Flew maintains quite boldly that 'The vision of God granted to men in Wesley's day was not equal to the revelation of Him in the first three Gospels, if it be true that God is what Jesus is, in his inexhaustible interest in human life', and then continues with Maltby:

> Our theological coat (says a modern Methodist) was cut for the figure of Total Depravity, but when it was tried on, it was found not to fit any kind of human nature. Accordingly we let out a seam in the back, as far as it would go, and the margin thus gained, with the stitches still showing, we called prevenient grace. Still the coat does not fit, for it is not by any afterthought that we can do justice to that boundless patience and holiness of God, which loves goodness everywhere, labours for it and delights in it everywhere. We have often thought of God as though it were 'all or nothing' with Him. But it is not true. In His mysterious humility He tends the last smouldering lamp in every rebellious heart. . . . It is He who defends the last strip of territory against the invasion of passion, when all the rest is gone, and raises mysterious defences about beleaguered virtues whose doom seemed sure. When He is denied or unrecognized in His own person, He still lingers about a man, dimly apprehended as a sense of duty, or as some indestructible principle, some notion of what is 'not cricket', some code of thieves, or He returns upon us in some New Thought, some shadowy Infinite, some impersonal Life-Force, some half-crazy system like Christian Science, worshipping its fragment of the truth— and so men entertain Him unawares. These vast tracts of the unbaptized human life we make over to poets, and

[1] Op. cit., 1965 edn., pp. 84–6.

novelists and dramatists, who explore them with inexhaustible interest and sympathy. Yet this interest and sympathy comes from God, Who loves this human life of ours, not only as a moralist approving where it is good, and disapproving where it is bad, but as a poet or artist loves it, because he cannot help loving a thing so strange, piteous and enthralling as the story of every human soul must be.[1]

METHODISM AND CATHOLICISM

It would be wrong to describe either Maltby or Findlay as a 'high-churchman', and the epithet is facile if applied to Flew in spite of his important work on the theology of the *ecclesia*. 'Fellowship Swanwick' did not promote Catholic-type retreats, and though the Sacrament of Holy Communion was reverently observed, it was not given disproportionate prominence. James Hope Moulton wrote a devotional book called *The Neglected Sacrament* in which he sought to redress the balance between the synoptic Eucharist and the Johannine *pedilavium*, which latter, he felt, was the necessary completion of the breaking of bread and pouring of wine. This would be congenial to many who later hung on Maltby's and Findlay's words. Findlay always interpreted the Lord's Supper by the 'comfortable words': 'Come unto me all ye that labour and are heavy-laden and I will give you rest.' It is interesting to speculate what he would think of any liturgical revision which left these out!

There were, however, Methodists who hungered for a much more definitely Catholic system. In 1933, at the time of the centenary of the Oxford Movement, R. N. Flew wrote an essay for the symposium edited by N. P. Williams on *Northern Catholicism*. It was called 'Methodism and the Catholic Tradition' and outlines, with admirable clarity and succinctness, the affinities between Methodism

[1] Op. cit., pp. 340–1.

and classic Christian spirituality. It makes for the first time some of the comparisons which have now become commonplaces when Methodists speak in ecumenical company, but are still not known among the generality of members.[1]

In the 1930s it became the fashion among some Methodists to stress these similarities, perhaps in ignorance of those other sources of Methodist devotion which are summarized in Chapter I above, and which later scholarship has uncovered. But the founding of the Methodist Sacramental Fellowship in 1935 was yet further evidence that Methodist spirituality was in need of a transfusion from the great Church, and that many felt that the piety of preaching, of extempore prayer, and of a somewhat jaded revivalism was like insipid soda water when they thirsted for the new wine of the Kingdom.

Long before the Methodist Sacramental Fellowship, a remarkable layman, former medical missionary, Sir Henry Lunn, had issued the first of three books of devotion, *The Love of Jesus* (1911), *Retreats for the Soul* (1913), and *The Secret of the Saints* (1933).

The first is specifically addressed to 'the people called Methodists'. Lunn contrasts the discipline and fervour of the mid-Victorian period with its meetings for prayer and quarterly fast days with the coldness of the new century. Here we have one of those jeremiads which were to re-echo throughout the connexion until the onset of the Second World War temporarily drowned them. 'We have deserted our first works and lost our love.' Lunn's solution was to stress the Catholic affinities of Methodism, to go back beyond Aldersgate Street to the Oxford Movement and the Holy Club. Offices, fasting and frequent communion are his remedies. He provides

[1] Op. cit. (London 1933), pp. 515-30.

simple offices for morning and evening, reserving confession for the night—an improvement perhaps on Cranmer
and the penitential tradition. There is, however, less use
of the Psalter than is traditional. Then follows Lancelot
Andrewes' Paraphrase of the Lord's Prayer, some devotions for every day of the week taken from Wesley,
Andrewes, à Kempis, and Prayers for the Christian Year
with particular concentration on Holy Week. There are
then extracts from Wesley's *A Companion for the Altar*,
abstracted, of course, from à Kempis, and a selection of
the hymns on the Lord's Supper. Lunn prints the whole of
the Communion Service, with prayers for use afterwards
and guides to Bible Study from the American Methodist
J. R. Mott, and to fasting from John Wesley. Archbishop
Cosmo Lang, who, though in some aspects prelatical and
pompous, had an interior life of deep devotion, said, in
1930, that he had used *The Love of Jesus* constantly.[1]

Retreats for the Soul has less Methodist reference and owes
more to post-Tridentine Catholicism. It is a book to
encourage the practice of withdrawal from the world for
periods of silent recollection. After some introductory
chapters on needs, history and methods, it consists of
spiritual writings, such as the *Preces Privatae* of Lancelot
Andrewes, the *Spiritual Combat* and the *Imitation of Christ*
arranged for use in retreat. There is also a selection of
sacred poetry, ranging from St Bernard through the
Carolines, the German mystics, Wesley, Keble and Faber,
to Evelyn Underhill. *The Practice of the Presence of God* is
included, doubtless to help the return to the kitchen sink
when the Retreat is over.

At the end, Lunn gives programmes of four retreats in
which he has shared. Two of them were for Methodists.
One, at Swanwick, in September, 1912, seems to have

[1] Henry S. Lunn, *The Secret of the Saints*, p. vii. For Lang see J. G. Lock-
hart, *Cosmo Gordon Lang* (1949).

been very much the kind of Conference-Retreat which is all that talkative Methodism has usually been able to manage; but the other, in June, 1913, was for Methodist undergraduates at Oxford and seems to have followed the genuine pattern, though conversation was allowed at meal times and from 11.30 a.m. to noon and from 2 p.m. to 4 p.m. each day, which adds up to a considerable amount.

It is doubtful if Lunn's second volume had much influence in his own communion, though it sold 8,000 copies in all; the word Retreat has been used increasingly in Methodism since about 1952, but the idea has rarely been grasped. Methodists as such do not understand or value silence; this is probably the defect of their virtue of friendliness and gregariousness.

The Secret of the Saints laments a further decline in the practice of prayer. A Committee on Corporate Prayer had been set up by the Wesleyan Conference of 1930 and had issued a questionary to Superintendent Ministers

> The following are some of the replies . . .: 'Prayer', says one 'is more a problem than a practice'. Another writes: 'The majority of Methodists have no interest in prayer'. Yet another says: 'I have come to the conclusion that Methodism, as I know it, has lost the desire for social prayer, and unlike Mr B—— I am both hopeless and helpless.'[1]

Lunn has no difficulty in showing that this is in complete contrast to the experience of the saints of all communions, and he reviews the history of prayer with tremendous insistence that the supreme occasion of corporate prayer is the Eucharist, and our private devotions should be related to this.

> From the prisons of Imperial Rome; from the solitary hermitages scattered along the banks of the Nile; from caves and castles under the blue skies of Italy and Spain;

[1] Op. cit., p. 5.

from the home of the Bishop of Geneva or the beautiful shores of the Lake of Annecy; from the torture chambers of the inquisition; from the tower of London; from Bedford jail; from the 'Temples of Silence' in Pennsylvania; from the little room in Aldersgate Street; from Oriel College and Hursley Vicarage there comes an ever-growing stream of testimony to the power of prayer, and an ever-increasing volume of lessons by which Our Lord and His Apostles of every age must answer our cry, 'Teach us to pray'.[1]

The Secret of the Saints is the most original of Lunn's trilogy, though, as the extensive bibliography shows, it is quarried from almost the whole of Christian spirituality. After the Introduction there are five chapters—'The Masters of Meditation', 'How to Pray', 'The Art of Meditation', 'The Discipline of Love', 'The Vision of God', the last drawing heavily on Kenneth Kirk's great Bampton Lectures of 1928. Then there are some concluding meditations and Gilbert Shaw's *A Pilgrim's Chapbook* as an appendix. The book is as truly catholic as Wesley's *Christian Library* which is part of its inspiration.

Lunn has some sympathetic pages on the Oxford Groups, which, in their pristine freshness of 1933, were doing much to revive the spiritual life in all communions, by offering the simple method of listening to God in the quietness in contrast to the overloaded techniques of the mystical manuals, and the agitated repetitious enthusiasms of the old-time prayer-meeting. Most spiritually sensitive Methodists found the Groups at this stage of great value, and were anxious to make available the positive insights of the movement. It was the developing extravagances in some of the groups, the disdainful attitude to the Church, the subjectivism of much of the guidance and the increasing heterodoxy and compromise with extreme political movements of the right, which led to disillusion. Of the

[1] Op. cit., p. 5.

theological inadequacy, J. Alexander Findlay had written in the very year of Lunn's third book:

> Sometimes, as I read about the Oxford groups, and feel the contagion of their new experience of God, I wonder; is a religion of success and power adequate for the world, or, for that matter for me? This new Oxford movement will only touch the fringe of the problem presented by the uneasy state of the modern Church, the desperate condition of the world, unless not merely Pentecost but Calvary, is in the heart of it. The only Pentecost which can really turn the world upside down is the Pentecost that shall follow a new vision of Calvary.[1]

Lunn's spirituality was a legitimate development from Wesley; but it did not represent popular Methodism and was likely to have more influence outside Methodism than within. There were many other Catholic Methodists during the '30s: T. S. Gregory, for instance, who was a great power in the Swanwick Schools of Fellowship, about whom Franciscan-type legends are extant in the circuits he served, and who became a Roman Catholic layman; and, somewhat senior, A. E. Whitham. On the latter's premature death in 1937 an unnamed correspondent—it could have been Sir Henry Lunn—wrote: 'There was much about him of the troubadour and more than a little of the Franciscan. There was in him a beautiful blend of goodness and gaiety. He was one of the gayest and most seriously religious persons I have ever met, and how he yearned to enter more deeply into the secret of the saints.'[2]

Whitham's sermons and articles, collected into volumes only after his death, are elegant pieces, devotional meditations, for the most part, of great insight, imagination and beauty. They are thoroughly sacramental and show how the masters of Catholic spirituality have become part of

---

[1] J. Alexander Findlay, *What did Jesus teach?* (London 1933), p. 212.
[2] A. E. Whitham, *The Discipline and Culture of the Spiritual Life* (1937), p. 9.

Whitham's Methodist soul. He tells of a vow he made during the war, that if he were spared he would strive for reconciliation with every enemy. 'Then I looked round to find my enemy. I had none among the nations—I was not a patriot of the imbecile order. I had not even a family relation I could call an enemy. But I had one, the Roman Catholic Church, which for me included High Church and Eastern Church. I had no fellowship with it: I had sought none. Here then was my business.'[1]

He then discovered that the large majority of the lovers of Jesus through the ages were on the side of 'the enemy'. 'It seemed a cynical thought that so many were so far astray, pasturing on poisoned herbs. I determined to read their best theology and devotional literature.'[2]

And here we make an unexpected discovery. The person to whom Whitham went for guidance in Catholic theology and devotion was Samuel Chadwick, Principal of Cliff College, and one of the most famed and intrepid evangelists of his day. 'Few people,' says Whitham, 'knew how wide a reader that stout apostle of Protestantism was, or how heartily he loved Catholic devotional manuals. He once confessed to me he always had a Catholic book of devotion in constant use on his table.'[3]

Chadwick's biographer provides further evidence of this. It may well have been the intensity of their prayers, which like Wesley with Lopez, drew Chadwick to the Catholics. His one great regret was that he had not prayed more. He revelled in the evangelicals George Muller and Hudson Taylor because they were men of prayer. But he confessed that if he had not been a Methodist he would have been a Roman Catholic, and that if the Lord permitted him to come into this world again and he could choose his sphere he would be the abbot of a

[1] A. E. Whitham, *The Discipline and Culture of the Spiritual Life* (1937), pp. 106–7.   [2] Ibid., p. 107.   [3] Ibid.

monastery. He loved the season of Lent. 'Lent requires sacrifice, devotion and prayer. These things may take worthless forms and then they are worthless, but they stand for deep spiritual necessities of the soul. That is why the six weeks of Lent should be so ordered as to give opportunity for concentration of heart and mind upon the Cross and Passion of our Lord Jesus Christ.'[1]

This shows that it is a mistake to look for the influences of Catholic devotion simply among the obvious high-churchmen and pioneers of ecumenism. Serious Christianity and deep devotion to Christ may unite men across the barriers of hierarchical system and ceremonial. Of this W. E. Sangster is a more recent instance to some extent outside our period. His book *The Pure in Heart* (1954) is astonishingly Catholic in its *exempla*.

Though the lure of Catholic spirituality for some Methodists was so strong, there was never so obvious a movement as that of the 'Free Catholics' of the Congregational and Unitarian Churches, men like W. E. Orchard and J. M. Lloyd Thomas.[2] No Methodist church was destined to house the pageantry of the Mass.

This may well have been due to the connexional system, which prevents ministers becoming isolated into eccentricity or parties, and even more, does not as a rule allow sufficient pulpit concentration for one man to be able to dictate the order of his Church's worship.

METHODISM AND PROTESTANTISM

The 1930s were the great period of the Catholic revival in Methodism when the Sacramental Fellowship was strongest and there were some defections to Rome. They were succeeded by a revival of Protestantism.

[1] Norman G. Dunning, *Samuel Chadwick* (London 1933), pp. 19–20.
[2] For a recent account see A. E. Peaston, *The Prayer Book Tradition in the Free Churches* (London 1964), pp. 171 ff.

It is important to notice this chronological order, which does not suit the propaganda of the pathologically sectarian and anti-Romans, who are always convinced that sacerdotalism has increased, is increasing and ought to be diminished. Dr R. N. Flew, who, as we have seen, was eager to expound the catholicity of Methodism, was also foster-father of the Protestant revival through his own knowledge of continental theology and the travelling scholars who went out from Wesley House, Cambridge. Thus did Karl Barth gain a hold in Methodism and the renowned Luther scholarship of Gordon Rupp and Philip Watson was born.

We must not minimize, either, the effect of the German Church struggle in which liberalism and the pale spirituality of the Oxford group type had seemed unable to discern the evil of Hitler or resist pagan myths of blood and race. There was a return to confessional orthodoxy.

In Methodism there was a rediscovery of Wesley, and particularly of 'our hymns'. Sometimes this was biased due to lack of ecumenical reference, as in Henry Bett's Fernley-Hartley lecture for 1937.[1] During the 1930s and 1940s there was a spate of books on hymnody, which, had they come earlier, could have saved the 1933 compilers from some of their less felicitous treatment of Wesley. Outstanding were the papers of the Congregationalist, Bernard Manning, *The Hymns of Watts and Wesley* (1942) and J. E. Rattenbury's Fernley-Hartley lecture for 1941, *The Evangelical Doctrines of Charles Wesley's Hymns*, to be followed in 1948 by his volume on *The Eucharistic Hymns of John and Charles Wesley*.

The 1940s were the age of Kenneth Kirk, Bishop of Oxford, and Dom Gregory Dix in the Church of England, and to their attempts to re-state the high Catholic

[1] *The Spirit of Methodism* (London 1937).

doctrines of orders and apostolic succession, Methodists, and Free Churchmen generally, were eager to oppose the splendour and true catholicity of their own heritage. Philip Watson's words are recent but they express the spirit of the '40s which set in motion considerable researches into Protestant spirituality.

It has more than once been alleged that Protestantism has produced 'no devotional literature'—a charge which on any showing is at least highly exaggerated. But naturally everything depends on what 'devotional literature' is supposed to be. If it is literature designed to foster 'the life of God in the soul of man'—to borrow with Wesley the title of a famous work of Puritan edification—then Protestantism has produced such literature in abundance and in large variety. Protestantism not only gave the Bible to the common man in his own tongue, but its scholars and theologians gave him commentaries on it, to assist him in applying its teaching to his life, and its preachers and teachers supplied him with printed sermons, tracts, and treatises on the spiritual life. They wrote and published journals describing their own spiritual pilgrimage for the help and encouragement of others; they gave personal spiritual counsel in letters; and they produced collections of hymns setting forth the doctrines of the faith and describing the varieties of spiritual experience. Such literature was available and was widely used, both by individuals privately and by family and other groups, through generation after generation of Protestants till the widespread decline of piety in recent times.[1]

None of this, however seems to have provided a satisfactory pattern of devotion for men and women in this

[1] *The Message of the Wesleys*, a reader of instruction and devotion compiled by Philip S. Watson (London 1965), pp. xiii–xiv. Perhaps it should be noted that Henry Scougal, author of *The Life of God in the Soul of Man*, was a Scottish Episcopalian and it is therefore debatable as to whether he should be classed as Puritan, though in the realm of guides to godliness such distinctions are notoriously difficult to sustain.

second half of the twentieth century. But in 1945, where our story ends at the end of the Second World War, Methodism was fairly confident of the future. The exigencies of war had placed a moratorium on self-criticism and demanded that nerves should be strong. There was little of the despair of Flew and his friends in 1917 or of our great depressions since. The Bible had come alive as though it were written for that hour. Orthodox Christianity, in its various confessional forms, now engaged in greater mutual co-operation and determined to set an example of unity to divided nations, seemed more than adequate for the conversion of England, if not the world. Methodism seemed to understand itself, its message and mission. With 'our hymns', 'our doctrines', 'our discipline', our organization and genius for fellowship, would we not prove to be once more in the vanguard of the warfare for men's souls? Would we not have uniquely precious gifts to bring to the great Church in its struggle for industrial society and its Divine task, which was peculiarly our own, of spreading Scriptural holiness throughout the world?[1]

[1] For examples of Methodist optimism from the pens of renowned scholars at this period, see the concluding paragraphs of A. W. Harrison's Wesley Historical Society lecture, *The Separation of Methodism from the Church of England* (London 1945); also, E. Gordon Rupp, *Principalities and Powers* (London 1952).

EPILOGUE: COLLAPSE AND RENEWAL?

THE mood of confidence in Methodism was not universal; and it was short-lived. Before long, there was talk of 'a dying Church' and by Coronation Year, 1953, Dr Sangster was openly wondering whether there was anything which would bring the British people back to God.

We have no right to assume, however, that Methodists today are any less devout than they have been for sixty years. They have less *pietas* in that they show little interest in the lives of their saints. Only the biography of a giant such as Sangster is likely to be a publishing success; it is doubtful if Bardsley Brash's study of his father would now exhaust five editions in twelve months as in 1913. But this apart, there has been ever more instruction in the life of prayer—though this is still not adequate—a greater demand for Conference-Retreats[1] if not for complete days of silence, a prayer-cell movement, which the dying Sangster began, and at least one book of devotion by a Methodist, David Head's *He Sent Leanness* (1959), which has its place among the few incisive and original manuals of our time. But although Methodism has greater resources than in its moods of despair it will allow, it is undergoing another 'crisis of identity', and a study of its spiritual tradition raises some acute problems. We can best consider them in the form of questions.

---

[1] The custom of a pre-ordination conference, with some attempt at silence, has been slowly introduced. Until recently Methodist ordinands were not even in such good case as those Anglicans whom the Bishop of Winchester ordained in 1885 at Farnham after a residential few days which made Charles Gore groan. See John Kent, *The Age of Disunity*, p. 147, n. 1.

1. *What is original in Methodist devotion?*

One is tempted to reply 'Wesley's synthesis, his amazing catholicity, which raided the treasury of the Christian ages, so far as it was available to him and invested it under Anglican-Puritan control'. But this does not do complete justice to Wesley's achievement or to the Methodist genius. He made men and women out of the common way free of this spirituality, the lower middle and working classes of two centuries, so that Thomas Collins could be familiar with the religious history of a Mexican hermit and a French nobleman, and Joseph Sutcliffe at the end of the eighteenth century and Samuel Chadwick at the beginning of the twentieth could love and admire Jesuit saints. The hymns echoed down the decades, brought very ordinary people to the gates of heaven and made one harmonious whole of private and public worship, rapt communion with God and aggressive evangelism, word and sacrament. In his essay on 'Methodism and the Catholic Tradition', R. Newton Flew tells a story recounted to him by a distinguished Anglican scholar, who had retired from a professorship to a country living. A woman in his parish was dying. 'One verse was constantly on her lips. She returned to it again and again.

> *Thy love I soon expect to find*
> *In all its depth and height;*
> *To comprehend the eternal mind*
> *And grasp the Infinite*

"What a magnificent verse", said the scholar, "for a peasant woman to die on!" It was to be found in a hymn "For believers seeking full redemption"; and on such hymns generations of ordinary believers have died, and by such hymns they have lived.'[1]

Had not Wesley provided such links with the Catholic

---

[1] *Northern Catholicism*, pp. 521–2.

faith, Methodism would have had no continuing life beyond the spasms of 'revival'. It might easily have become the prey of cranks, Adventists and 'enthusiasts'. As it was, his legacy was handed on, and, at any time, as Flew and Lunn so remarkably showed, a recall of Methodism to its first works was a summons, not to a narrow sectarianism but to the ample glories of the Holy Catholic Church. Add to this the fact that so many ordinary Methodists, like Bunyan's three or four poor women in Bedford 'spake as if Joy did make them speak'.[1] and you have a spiritual phenomenon remarkable in Church history.

2. *To what extent did Methodism through the years lose Wesley's catholicity?*

Never completely; but its reluctant assertion of its churchmanship after Wesley's death and its not unnatural suspicions of Catholic Anglicanism after the Oxford Movement combined to deprive it of a worship equal to its spirituality. This has made it difficult to relate teaching about prayer and the Sacraments to what actually happens in the Sunday service of the average Methodist church. Had the Sunday morning Eucharist of the Wesleys been continued, had the Book of Common Prayer, with the Wesley hymns, been the staple food of all the Societies, there might have been realized in the Victorian Age the type of church of which the ecumenical vision of our time sees and greets from afar. Perhaps this was impossible in any case; the gulf between Anglicans and Methodists—social more than theological—was too great. And the nineteenth century was the age of liberty and invididualism, asserted in division rather than comprehensiveness. It was, as much for Roman and Anglo-Catholics as for Methodists, an age in which liturgy was simply not understood.

[1] J. Bunyan, *Grace Abounding*, 38.

The more ponderable decline in the nineteenth century was due to a fear of the world, a retreat into the connexion, a refusal to come honestly to terms with the scientific revolution (in spite of Dallinger), the defensive mentality of 'The Christian answer to ——' (which is still with us), and a loss of certain elements of Wesley, especially his seventeenth-century Anglican heritage, for instance, the Cambridge Platonists. The Caroline Divines were made over to the Anglo-Catholic Library. As Gordon Rupp once said 'The old Methodist frame was breaking up and in some ways Victorian nonconformity had narrower horizons than the old Arminian Catholicity. Jabez Bunting's lucid sermons are the last great exposition of Justification by Faith: thereafter the preaching of the cross is split into an abstract doctrine of Atonement on the one hand and an emotional crisis of conversion on the other. William Arthur's *Tongue of Fire* apart, it seems that the doctrines of the Spirit and of Perfect Love were left to those who, under the influence of new revival movements would equate Scriptural holiness with fundamentalist pietism.'[1]

There was a failure, which, needless to say many Anglicans shared, to appreciate such a prophet as Frederick Denison Maurice. Younger men like John Scott Lidgett and Hugh Price Hughes saw the importance of his theology and were wise in their generation, but even they were beguiled into the abortive venture of Free Church federalism, which was not Methodism's providential way especially at a time when the Reformed tradition tended to be submerged by pulpiteering and there was no genuine moral theology, only the nonconformist conscience.

3. Was Wesley's own system of spirituality altogether viable?
Ronald Knox said, with more exactness than in some of

[1] E. Gordon Rupp, *Methodism and the Protestant Tradition* (London 1951), pp. 25–6.

the remarks of his scintillating chapters on Wesley that 'his ideal did not fall short of persuading 70,000 people to adopt, for all practical purposes, the rules of the Holy Club'.[1] To study the *Directions Given to the Band Societies*, dated Christmas Day, 1744, is to wonder if this in some articles is not a spirituality too austere for all but a few. R. N. Flew has sorrowfully recounted some sorry examples of the early Methodist attitude to art, the self-suspicion even of Wesley if he found himself taking time off to enjoy architecture or the exhibits of the British Museum. As for his preacher, John Pawson, he burnt Wesley's copy of Shakespeare, with all Wesley's copious notes.[2]

Methodism has become a great Church but it has, in spite of disclaimers, made too much of the parity of vocation and religious experience with the result that is has not sufficiently provided for the infinite varieties of temperament, some worldly by the more intense standards and yet not without some capacity to respond to the love of God and not beyond some place in his Church. It was for this that Maltby, Flew and Findlay were contending.[3]

But there is a question more radical still:

4. *Are the traditional Christian disciplines at all relevant today? Do not we need entirely new patterns of spirituality for 'secular saints'?*

Many Christians are in revolt against classic piety both Catholic and Protestant. Part of the rebellion is 'Protestant' in that it is an extension of Kierkegaard's attack on Christendom and Barth's insistence that 'Religion is not

[1] R. A. Knox, *Enthusiasm* (Oxford 1950), p. 432.
[2] R. N. Flew, *The Idea of Perfection in Christian Theology*, p. 339.
[3] See the remarkable article by J. A. Findlay in *The Preachers' Quarterly*, December 1954, 'Can we be "Friends of Sinners" and yet separate from them?', in which he confesses 'I had lost something by becoming a Methodist Minister' (i.e. his ability to help 'sinners') and tells how Irish R.C. priests, by sharing drinks, were able to point some of the 'lost' to the Saviour.

Salvation'. Some of the protagonists are high churchmen, who seem, like Luther, to have forced themselves into ways of devotion unsuited to their natures, which have not only become burdens too grievous to be borne but have protected them from the Living God.[1]

Others feel that the ordered life of traditional piety is completely unsuited to the modern world. The rhythm of life in automated industrial society makes nonsense of the monastic hours or even of Matins and Evensong and Lancelot Andrewes' *Dial*. Neither is Brother Lawrence's kitchen at all like that of the modern housewife with its innumerable gadgets, but also its children at play. Devotional discipline is a churchly activity which involves retreat into a pietistic cocoon, insulated from the real world of science, art and politics, warring races and hungry peoples, bingo and brothels and electric guitars. Jesus-piety whether Bernardine or 'liberal' is either palely or erotically sentimental and cannot withstand Gospel criticism.

Others again, go so far as to claim that linguistic philosophy has made belief in a personal God untenable. So, much of prayer is thereby nullified.[2]

On all this, I would make but two brief, concluding comments, though I would not be thought unaware of the necessity of reconstruction of the theology of prayer. (1) There could be a real danger that the Christians who lead this revolt are too much at the mercy of prevailing philosophical fashion. Empiricism, the belief that only what is verified in experience can be true, has, in one form or another, been dominant these last twenty years, while metaphysics, the attempt to give a systematic

[1] Cf. John Robinson, *Honest to God* (1963), and H. A. Williams in *Objections to Christian Belief*, ed. A. R. Vidler (London 1963), pp. 35 ff.

[2] See Mark Gibbard, 'Christian Spirituality: the Contribution of the Communities', *London Quarterly and Holborn Review*, January 1966, pp. 25 ff.

explanation of the universe and to discover a transcendent purpose which all things serve, has been largely abandoned. But there is no guarantee that this is more than one of the passing phases of thought. It would seem somewhat doubtful whether human life can long continue without some transcendental reference, and although religionless Christianity is possible as a system of ethics without more than a symbolic or mythical theology, it involves repudiating much of the teaching of Jesus, and is not likely to win the allegiance of more than a few semi-Christian pseudo-intellectuals.[1]

(2) Those who revolt so strongly against the old disciplines of devotion (and what was said in criticism of Wesley and Methodism could be taken as part agreement with them) seem to recognize that some mental activity of withdrawal and detachment from the world is necessary, some opportunity to see life steadily and see it whole. Meditation is the one classical activity not altogether inimical to worldly holiness; but once this is granted, intercession, even if in the reduced sense of thinking of our friends before Ultimate Reality, is not likely to be omitted. The simple faith that my importunity may change the whole course of nature and of history by summoning Divine intervention, is very hard to sustain in a scientific age. But the influence of mind upon mind is still an unsolved mystery, and if we must be agnostic about the Divine Omnipotence, it is not naïve to regard prayer as one of the means whereby we become fellow-workers with God. Pascal's dictum that God

[1] Epicureanism is a parallel from the ancient world, an irreligious, though noble philosophy since it disclaims all possibility of co-operation with a universal purpose.

> Nothing to fear from God
> Nothing to feel 'neath the sod.
> Evil can be endured.
> Good can be secured.

instituted prayer to teach his creatures the dignity of causality is profoundly religious and not incompatible with empirical philosophy, for that matter.

That we need saints does not require to be argued, except to make the inevitable qualification that a saint is no delicate object of unreal piety from a stained-glass window, but a strong, dedicated and perhaps rugged servant of mankind. In an age when science and the prevailing philosophy, and the very need to control the teeming resources of nature, which otherwise might overwhelm us, may condition us to a dull, mechanised uniformity (hygienic but incapable of inspiration), and make the world safe for daleks, the Church must recover its mission as a school of prayer. In 1933, Sir Henry Lunn quoted words of John Wesley, written to Alexander Mather on 6 August, 1777, which are more than ever pertinent: 'Give me one hundred preachers who fear nothing but sin and desire nothing but God, and I care not a straw whether they be clergymen or laymen, such alone will shake the gates of hell and set up the kingdom of heaven upon earth.'[1]

To give such confidence and quicken such desire, we shall need all the experience of the great Christian traditions as well as the fresh truth and light which God has to impart. The study of Methodist devotion should be of present help as well as of historic interest, not because God repeats himself[2] or old forms can be made to fit new needs, but because love for the past kindles our faith in the communion of saints and helps to give us compassion and tolerance in this world and a hunger and thirst for the eternal kingdom, without which not only our prayers but our lives would lose their full meaning.

[1] Henry S. Lunn, *The Secret of the Saints*, p. 67.
[2] The moving story of the Negro crying out before the memorial plaque to William Booth, 'Do it again, Lord', shows in some sense a misunderstanding of the doctrine of the Holy Spirit.

INDEX

PROPER NAMES

Adams, Thomas, 39
à Kempis, Thomas, 22, 43, 100
Allchin, A. M., 23n., 26n., 28, 29n., 32n.
Alleine, Joseph, 38
Alleine, Richard, 38
Alstyne, Frances Jane van, 68n.
Andrewes, Lancelot, 28, 100
Andrews, J. H. B., 54n.
Arthur, William, 61–6, 69, 81, 112
Asbury, Francis, 57
Atmore, Charles, 71
Augustine (Austin), 26, 34, 71, 76

Baptism (*see* Sacraments)
Barratt, T. H., 49n.
Barth, Karl, 106
Basil of Caesarea, 26
Baxter, Richard, 35–7, 38, 70
Bayly, Lewis, 78
Beckerlegge, O. A., 48n., 51
Bernard of Clairvaux, 34, 100
Bett, Henry, 31, 106
Beyond the Fringe, 83
Bourignon, Antoinette, 32
Bourne, Hugh, 56ff.
Bowmer, J. C., 49n.
Bownde, Nicholas, 78
Brash, J. Denholm, 69n., 86
Brash, W. Bardsley, 109
Bright, William, 20
Brightman, F. E., 28n.
Bunting, Jabez, 55, 112
Bunting, T. P., 55n.
Bunting, W. M., 78
Bunyan, John, 28, 64, 69, 111n.
Burns, Robert, 73–4
Butler, Cuthbert, 34, 46

Calvert, James, 48
Camp, Meeting, 57ff.
Carmelites, 30
Catholics, Roman, 30
Cell, G. C., 38

Chadderton, Laurence, 61
Chadwick, Samuel, 104–5, 110
Champness, Thomas, 68
Chapman, J. Arundel, 18
Chrysostom, 26
Church, L. F., 35n., 38n.
Clarke, Adam, 32, 52
Class Leaders Assistant, 86–7
Cliff College, 21, 68, 104
Clowes, William, 46f.
Coley, Samuel, 44n., 54n., 74n., 80n.
Collins, Thomas, 39, 44ff., 60, 74, 110
Common Prayer, Book of, 14, 23, 37, 47, 52, 83
Covenant, Service, 21, 45, 71
Cowper, William, 87

Dakin, J. F. C., 86n.
Dallinger, W. H., 85–6, 112
Davies, Rupert E., 22n.
Deissmann, Adolf, 18
de Renty, Count Gaston Jean-Baptiste, 30ff., 39, 44
de Sales, François, 32
Dix, Gregory, 107
Doddridge, Philip, 21, 38
Donne, John, 24
Dow, Lorenzo, 56ff.
Drake, Richard, 28n.
Dunning, Norman G., 105n.
Dutton, W. E., 51n.

Edwards, Jonathan, 71
Exercises, Ignatian, 39n.

Fathers, Early, 24, 25f.
Fathers, Greek, 22
Fellowship of the Kingdom, 90
Fenélon, 32
Findlay, J. A., 63n., 90, 92, 95–6, 103, 113
Fletcher, John, 33–4

Flew, R. Newton, 11, 16, 18, 26n., 33, 69n., 86, 90, 91, 92, 95–8, 106, 108, 110–11
Fox, George, 28n.
Francis of Assisi, 35
Francke, Sebastian, 32

George, A. Raymond, 11, 83n.
Gerhardt, Paul, 33
Gibbard, Mark, 114n.
Goodwin, Thomas, 39
Green, Richard, 85
Greg, Samuel, 20
Gregory, The Great, 34
Gregory of Nyssa, 26
Gregory, T. S., 103
Group Movement, Cambridge, 90
Group movement, Oxford, 14, 21, 102–3, 106
Guild, Wesley, 21
Guyon, Madam, 32

Haime, John, 37
Hall, Joseph, 35
Harris, Howel, 42
Harrison, A. W., 108n.
Head, David, 109
Heiler, Friedrich, 35
Herbert, George, 70
Hewitson, Isaac, 63n.
Heywood, Oliver, 71
Hildebrandt, Franz, 27n.
Hill, Richard, 33–4
Hodges, H. A., 23n., 26n., 29n., 32n.
Homilies, 25
Hooker, Richard, 24
Hughes, Hugh Price, 112
Hunter, John, 21
Hymns on the Lord's Supper, 20, 25

Inge, Paula, 76n.
Inge, W. R., 76n.

Jackson, Thomas, 52
Jaeger, H., 32n.
Johnson, Howard, 24
Jones, Elizabeth E., 75
Jones, James B., 75–6
Julian of Norwich, 28, 40, 86

Kempe, Margery, 40
Ken, Thomas, 24

Kendall, H. B., 55n.
Kent, John, 53n., 84–5
Kirk, K. E., 102, 106–7
Knowles, David, 28
Knox, Alexander, 43
Knox, R. A., 32n., 112–13

Lang, Cosmo, 100
Law, William, 22, 24, 32, 33, 43
Lawrence, Brother, 114
Lax, W. H., 79
Leys School, Cambridge, 78
Library, The Christian, 22, 31, 36, 102
Lidgett, J. Scott, 92, 112
Lightfoot, R. H., 92
London Quarterly and Holborn Review, 18n., 21n., 51n., 114n.
London Quarterly Review, 49n.
Lopez, Gregory, 30ff., 34–5, 40, 44, 104
Lord's Day (see Sabbath)
Lord's Supper (see Sacraments)
Love Feasts, 21, 41, 47, 71, 89
Loyola, Ignatius, 53
Lunn, Henry S., 99–103, 111, 116
Lyte, H. F., 52

'Macarius the Egyptian', 26, 67
Maltby, W. R., 90ff., 113
Maltby, T. R., 91n., 94n.
Manning, Bernard L., 14–15, 27, 106
McAdoo, H. R., 82n.
McCaughey, Davies, 92
Methodist, Bible Christians, 54
Methodist Magazine, 86n.
Methodists, Oxford, 23, 49
Methodists, Primitive, 46, 56–60
Methodists, Sacramental Fellowships, 99, 105
Methodists, School of Fellowship, 90
Methodists, United Methodist Free Churches, 48n.
Methodists, Wesleyan, 14, 54, 55
Methodists, Quaker, 59
Middleton, Conyers, 25
Missionaries, 47–8
Molinos, Michael, 32
Moffatt, James, 27
Montgomery, James, 19
Moravians, 25, 33
Morgan, Irvonwy, 18n.

Mott, J. R., 100
Moulton, J. H., 91, 98

Nelson, John, 46f.
Nelson, Robert, 24, 71
Nettleton, Joseph, 48n.
Newton, John A., 39n.
Newton, John, 79
Niebuhr, Reinhold, 65
Non-Jurors, 24
Northcott, Hubert, 64
Nuttall, G. F., 42n., 59f.

Orchard, W. E., 105
Orcibal, Jean, 22, 32n., 34n.
Ouseley, Gideon, 69
Outler, Albert C., 22, 30, 32n., 34
Oxford Movement, 51–2

Palmer, Phoebe, 67
Pascal, B., 115–16
Pawson, John, 113
Peake, A. S., 91
Peaston, A. E., 105n.
Peters, Mary, 86–7
Plan of Pacification, 49
Pourrat, Philippe, 9
Prayer Meeting, 21, 56
'Praying William', 50–1, 69, 74, 79
Preston, John, 18, 38
Punshon, W. M., 80
Puritans, 37ff., 71ff.
Pusey, E. B., 28

Quakerism, 59ff.

Rack, Henry D., 85n., 86n.
Ramsey, A. M., 37n.
Rattenbury, J. Ernest, 16 n., 29, 106
Rawlinson, A. E. J., 92
Reformers, English, 33
Richardson, Alan, 92
Robinson, John A. T., 114n.
Robson, G. B., 21
Routley, Erik, 81
Rupp, E. Gordon, 22n., 27n., 30, 106, 108n., 112
Sabbath, 39, 78–80

Sangster, W. E., 86, 105, 109
Schmidt, Martin, 32n., 40
Scougal, Henry, 107n.
Shaw, Gilbert, 102
Shubotham, Daniel, 56, 58
Smith, Timothy L., 67
Smyth, Charles, 28n.
Song of Songs, 17f.
Southlands College, 79
Spinckes, Nathaniel, 24
Spooner, George, 77
Spooner, W. H. (my grandfather), 10, 72ff. 85, 89
Stennett, Joseph, 38
Stranks, C. J., 78n.
Studia Liturgica, 11
Sunday (see Sabbath)
Sutcliffe, Joseph, 53n., 110
Symeon, the New Theologian, 28–9
Symeon, the Pious, 29

Taylor, Hudson, 104
Taylor, Jeremy, 22, 24, 43, 96
Telford, John, 37n.
Tersteegen, Gerhard, 33
Theologia Germanica, 33
Thomas, J. M. Lloyd, 105
Thornton, Martin, 40n.
Tillich, Paul, 40n.
Tinsley, E. J., 35n.
Tripp, David, 21n.
Tyerman, Luke, 50, 69n.

Walsh, J. D., 71–2
Watson, Philip S., 106–7
Watts, Isaac, 38 57
Weatherhead, Leslie D., 63n., 90, 95
Wesley, Charles, 10, 14, 16f., 23, 29, 33, 34, 37, 42, 46, 57, 73, 76, 94, 106
Wesley, John, 13, 21, 22–43, 44, 69, 71, 95, 106, 110ff.
Wesley, Susannah, 39, 87
Whitham, A. E., 103–4
Wilkinson, John T., 36n., 37n., 47n., 59
Williams, H. A., 114n.
Williams, N. P., 98
Wilson, D. Dunn, 32n.

Xavier, Francis, 53

SUBJECTS

Anglicanism, 23ff., 49

Band Meeting, 42

Church Consciousness, 48–54
Class Meeting, 10, 20–1, 31, 41f.,
    71, 89
Conscience, 10, 29
Counter-Reformation, 30, 32

Epicureanism, 115n.

Family, The, 71–80
Fasting, 24, 45, 70

Holy Trinity, Prayer to, 44, 45
Hymns, 14ff., 46, 48, 52, 58, 76–7,
    94, 106, 110

Mysticism, 14ff., 23, 32ff., 45–7

Preaching, 39, 80–4

Reason, 24
Retreats, 100f., 109
Revivalism, 54–71

Sacraments, Baptism, 13, 14, 63
Sacraments, Lord's Supper, 19, 49–
    51, 63, 111
Sanctification Entire, 21
'Second Blessing', 21, 67
Spirituality, 9ff., 22, 29

Theology, Dogmatic, 9
Theology, Federal, 39
Theology, Moral, 9
Theology, Spiritual, 9